DATE			

BRIGHT PROMISE

Donita Dyer

ZONDERVAN
PUBLISHING HOUSE
OF THE ZONDERVAN CORPORATION
GRAND RAPIDS, MICHIGAN 49506

Bright Promise
Copyright © 1983 by The Zondervan Corporation

Library of Congress Cataloging in Publication Data
Dyer, Donita.
    Bright promise.
      1. Yang, Chung Syn, 1920–   . 2. Blind—Korea—Biography. I. Title.
HV1624.Y36D92   1983   362.4'1'0924 [B]   83-1203
ISBN 0-310-45751-3

Edited by Evelyn Bence and Julie Ackerman Link
Designed by Kim Koning

Printed in the United States of America

83 84 85 86 87 88 89 90 / 9 8 7 6 5 4 3 2

To the people of America, with love and gratitude. From the bottom of my heart I thank you for sending missionaries, money, and men to help liberate our country and bring new hope through Jesus Christ our Lord.

Chung Syn Yang, M.D.

Thanks to Dr. Henry Syn who translated Chung Syn Yang's Braille notes into English. Without his diligence and devotion this book would not be possible.

Donita Dyer

Contents

Introduction

Incredible! How else can one describe Dr. Chung Syn Yang? This amazing physician, educator, and theologian believes she can do all things through Christ who gives her strength. A long list of astounding accomplishments proves the point!

Chung Syn was raised in Korea at a time when blind children such as herself were rejected, scorned, and unschooled. Yet this courageous child overcame handicaps then with the same kind of determination, resourcefulness, and faith in God that enables her to conquer challenges today.

Before starting this inspiring true story let's take a quick look at Chung Syn's people, their culture, and their paradoxical country.

Korea, a picturesque, mountainous peninsula, is six hundred miles long and approximately 135 miles wide. The small country extends into the Yellow Sea on the west and is bordered on the north by Manchuria. The Sea of Japan sweeps over it eastern shores.

Through the years Korea's fertile valleys, peaceful plains, and ancient cities repeatedly flared into battle, being invaded by China and Japan on numerous occasions. In 1895, Korea became an absolute monarchy, but independence was short-lived. Like bees in search of nectar, greedy neighbors swarmed over the country in 1905.

Since Korea (translated Chosen, or Cho'sun) was no match

for the Imperialist Army, Japan's conquest ended quickly. Occupation forces took over, and during a forty-year reign of terror, authorities stripped the conquered populace of its national identity—but not of its dignity. Korean students were taught to read, write, and speak Japanese, and a mandate was issued requiring them to worship at Shinto shrines. Some complied; others refused. The latter, called "stiff necks," received severe reprisals.

The outside world knew little of what was going on, nor did it seem to care. Korea, the immortal "Land of Morning Calm," was still an enigma to many, its Confucian ethics and quaint oriental customs setting it apart from the West. Following World War II, however, Korea changed dramatically. With peace came independence and a resurgence of national pride. Aggressive and ambitious young leaders took over the reins, attempting to unify the country; but their efforts failed. Following the Korean War this nation was divided, and today the north is under communist control.

The Republic of South Korea, in spite of newly acquired technology and sophistication, is still a curious composite of old and new—a page out of the past, yet a panorama of today's progress and a bold declaration of things to come.

A short drive through the countryside gives one a glimpse of the Korea Chung Syn knew as a child—the rural areas have been slow to change. Farming families live simply. Many still follow in the footsteps of past generations: mothers plant and cultivate with babies tied on their backs; fathers take their produce to market in ox carts or carry it in A-frames slung across their backs.

All available land is cultivated. Even terraced mountain slopes produce food for the nation's mushrooming metropolises. But since fish provide much of the protein for Korean tables, men who harvest the seas are as indispensable to the national economy as rice farmers.

Springtime is spectacular in Korea. When winter snows melt and trickle down the slopes, hills comes alive with greenery. Grain fields sprout, fruit orchards blossom, and distant mountain peaks disappear mysteriously into the morning mist. Such scenes charm visitors, but those acquainted with history realize that this nation is more than a picturesque land of enchantment. Young men and old men—yes, even women and children—have sacrificed to protect and preserve the "Land of Morning Calm." Is it any wonder that today each mountain peak and plain is a symbol of strength, perseverance, and endurance?

To thoroughly understand a nation one must first feel the pulse of its people. What are their roots? What has formulated their traditions? How do they think and feel?

Koreans are of the Mongolian race, but historians and linguists disagree as to their ancestral beginning. Some say they are an amalgamation of Ainu, Japanese, and Chinese. Others contend their ancestors migrated from Manchuria and southern Siberia long before Japan existed as a nation, and their features do suggest a subtle blend of both oriental and occidental.

As a nationality Koreans are extremely intelligent, ambitious, tenacious, and resourceful. Steeped for centuries in the ethics of Confucianism theirs has been a filial-oriented society. For the oldsters, life was contemplative, simple, and serene, the social structure based on simple premises: king over subjects, father over sons, elder over younger, and husband over wife. Since there was no national social security system, elder sons supported their parents, each family caring for its own members.

Korean food is as colorful and contrasting as the country itself, ranging from subtly bland to highly spiced, from mild to peppery hot. Korea's national dish, in addition to traditional rice, is a highly seasoned cabbage called *kimchi*. Also familiar to westerners is *bulgogi,* thinly sliced barbecued beef strips cooked at the table on charcoal braziers. For the visitor, dining in the "Land of Morning Calm" can be an epicurean delight.

While Korea embraces many creeds it claims no state religion per se, although Buddhism is perhaps the most widely practiced faith. Originally imported from China and India, the ancient religion later became perverted by shamanism, thus embracing the worship of ancestral spirits. Other superstitions also played a part in early rites with devil's posts erected outside village gates to frighten away demons.

Sometime during the nineteenth century, Christianity was introduced to the people of Korea, helping to change superstitious concepts. Due to Western influence Christianity has become a viable and growing faith. Churches dot both the cities and the rural countryside. At one of these small Presbyterian churches Chung Syn became a youthful follower of the Lord Jesus Christ.

The Republic of South Korea's current independence and prosperity is indeed a tribute to perseverance and resiliency. Neither imperialism nor communism, not even civil war, has been able to discourage or prevent this country from achieving its national goals. No doubt it is this same persistence and pride that has enabled Korea's sons and daughters to pursue personal dreams and to translate them into reality.

Here, in this *Chosen* country, Chung Syn Yang was born. These are her people! These are her roots!

My own life has been greatly challenged by Dr. Yang's courage and commitment. I trust her autobiography, the incredible story of a diminutive woman with a towering list of accomplishments, will inspire and enrich the lives of all who read it.

CHAPTER 1

Bright Promise

Faint rays of sunlight crept across the horizon. A cock crowed, and Soon-yul rose from her pallet to prepare breakfast. Slowly and deliberately she moved about the small kitchen, knowing that her father-in-law and his men were impatient to leave for the mountain.

Later that morning when the last bowl was washed, Soon-yul stood by the window and watched her daughter carry a basketful of dried fish and rice cakes up the trail for the woodcutters' lunch. She had intended to go herself—until severe pains left her cringing and clinging to the table for support.

She would soon give birth to another child! Soon-yul smiled with satisfaction; her secret was safe. No one suspected that her delivery was near. Good! She had to see this through alone!

Fighting a wave of fear and panic, Soon-yul lay down once more. Outside everything seemed at peace. Sunshine drenched the day, although a certain crispness in the air warned of winter weather ahead. In the distance, purple-streaked mountains stood like sentinels behind rice paddies, and sleepy settlements sprawled along the slopes below. Each detail was familiar. This was Korea—her homeland!

Before the Japanese occupation, life had been tranquil. Since that dreadful day in the spring of 1920, however, many changes had disrupted and divided the House of Yang. Before her husband had gone into hiding, he had sold their home. Now she and the children lived in poverty. Her days were filled with work and worry. Would her husband ever return?

Soon-yul tossed and turned on the thin straw pallet in an effort to ease the pain. Disturbing fears flashed through her mind, and she tried to shove them aside.

"Sihwal, where are you?" she sobbed, calling out for the father of her unborn child. "Please come home. The children and I need you, Sihwal. Now!"

Outside she could hear the noises of nature—doves calling to their mates; the family dog barking at passers by; cart wheels clattering along dusty roads. Inside the tiny cottage, only her own voice broke the silence. It seemed to mock her as it echoed through the empty house and ricocheted off bare walls.

Sihwal, her beloved, was somewhere in Russia hiding from the Japanese military police. He had left her in Korea to care for the family and to give birth to their fifth child—alone.

For months doubts had tormented her. Could she continue working in the fields? Even now their diet was much too meager. Could she harvest the rice crop without help? And what about fuel? That very morning she had burned the last straw and twigs to cook breakfast. How could she gather and cut firewood? How could she keep the drafty cottage warm when winter winds whistled through the flimsy doors and windows?

The girls' dresses were patched and thin, the soles of their straw sandals worn through. They had managed to get by during the summer, but how could they walk in the snow without shoes?

Added to Soon-yul's humiliation was the painful knowledge that she had disgraced the House of Yang by producing only daughters. If only this baby were a man-child, she would find favor with her in-laws and bring pleasure to Sihwal. She would gain new stature in the eyes of her neighbors as well.

Each contraction reinforced her earlier decision. Come what may, she would deliver this child alone, without the assistance of her unsympathetic mother-in-law. Even now the thought of Mother Yang's barbed remarks brought stinging tears to her eyes. "Another worthless girl," the older woman had taunted at the birth of her last granddaughter. "Can't you do better than that? Who will carry on the family name after we're gone?" Her father-in-law had shared his wife's sentiments, and Sihwal had looked at his wife with reproachful eyes.

Every corner of Soon-yul's brain was crowded with memories, painful memories that haunted her at times such as this. She remembered each detail of the day when Sihwal had told her he was leaving home. She had listened in stunned silence, too shocked at first to react or understand the meaning of his words.

"Pack my heaviest clothes, Soon-yul," he had instructed. "I'm going sardine fishing soon."

"But this is spring," she protested. "Why do you need warm clothes?"

Sihwal avoided his wife's gaze. "The military police know of my underground activities; they plan to arrest me." He cleared his throat before continuing. "Today I bought a fishing boat."

"How? Where did you get the money?"

"I . . . I sold the house," he mumbled. "But don't worry.

My nets should turn a tidy profit. We'll buy another place when I come home."

"What about the girls and me?"

"Deacon Chang says you can move into the cottage by the prayer chapel. It's not much, but you'll have a roof over your heads." Soon-yul stifled a sob and her husband's voice softened. "If the new baby is a boy, take good care of him, won't you?"

"And if it's another girl?"

He shrugged his shoulders and answered impulsively. "Give her away if you like . . . to some childless couple." The words were spoken kindly, but heard as a caustic and painful rebuke.

With a heavy heart she helped him pack. Four days later, after tearful farewells, Sihwal shouldered his knapsack and sprinted down the dirt trail. He turned to wave, then quickly disappeared from view. No news had arrived until the previous week. His letter had been postmarked Moscow, Russia.

Another sharp and shattering contraction brought Soon-yul's thoughts back to the challenge at hand. With fists tightly clenched, she proceeded with the delivery, more determined than ever to go through with her cunning plans. *If this child is a female,* she resolved, *I will destroy it—and kill myself! My shame and disgrace will be over before anyone discovers what I have done. Without Sihwal, life isn't worth the struggle.*

Finally the head appeared, no more than a tiny ball of matted fuzz. Soon-yul's fingers touched it with tenderness. Maternal instincts instantly roused. She envisioned a strong, healthy son—a man-child to make Sihwal's chest swell with pride. But soon the squirming, slippery infant lay in her hands. One frantic glance confirmed her original fears: another daughter!

Soon-yul's courage faltered, but only for a second. Quickly

she severed the cord and stifled the small inner voice that cried, "Don't destroy her! You can't do this! Your daughter has a right to live!" She slipped the newborn beneath her straw pallet to muffle its lusty screams. Then, physically and emotionally drained, Soon-yul collapsed.

When Mother Yang approached the cottage a short time later, she was greeted with sounds of weeping and moaning. She stopped. Had another girl been born? Was her dream of a healthy, handsome grandson again dashed? Tears blinding her, she stumbled away from the cottage and toward her own home, disappointed and fearful that she had been denied the longed-for grandson. Suddenly, not fully realizing why, the woman turned and retraced her steps, then hurried inside.

With a single swoop Mother Yang's eyes took in the scantily furnished room. "Soon-yul, where is the child?" she screamed. "Is it not enough that you have disgraced our family? Must you add murder to your sins?" Noticing a lump under the young woman's pallet she dropped to her knees and uncovered a tiny infant gasping for breath. Moved by the child's struggle to survive, the old woman cuddled the blue baby in her arms, warming the small body close to her breast.

The very next morning Soon-yul returned to work in a neighbor's field, leaving thirteen-year-old Sunbi with the baby. Sunbi carried the infant on her back, papoose-style, while doing the household chores, and days later, when their mother was confined to bed with a raging fever, she fed her sister rice water from a spoon.

Lovingly, and with maternal devotion far beyond her years, Sunbi cared for her baby sister, who gurgled and cooed with delight whenever she received the slightest attention. Even their mother at times marveled at the beauty of her daughter's dark, smiling eyes.

When winter stepped aside, giving way to variegated greens

and blue skies, Soon-yul's fever passed. She returned to the fields. Her baby, although small for her age, childishly exuded a love for life.

One starlit night Soon-yul lay awake. She had worked in the rice paddies all day; every muscle cried out for rest, yet her nerves were taut, like live wires, and her eyes were sleepless. *How much longer can I carry on?* she wondered. *Has Sihwal forgotten me? Will he take another wife when he learns I have given birth to a fifth girl? Will he blame me?*

Around midnight Soon-yul heard footsteps, followed by scratching sounds at the front door. Horrified, she watched a hand reach in and attempt to unlatch the hook. Quickly she grabbed a board used for ironing and crouched in the shadows. The latch lifted. The door swung open. A dark shadow stepped inside, and Soon-yul raised her arm to strike the intruder.

"Is this the way you welcome your husband home?" a familiar voice asked as he clasped her in his arms. Tears of happiness and thanksgiving flooded Soon-yul's face. Her husband looked thin and tired, his clothes dirty and ragged. But he was home. Nothing else mattered.

Sihwal told her he'd lost his boat. He had hoped to find asylum in Russia, but the country was embroiled in revolution. Conditions there were even more desperate than in Korea. Little children, many scarcely past the toddling stage, were begging for food in the streets. Seeing them made him think of his own family. Eager to return, he made friends with merchants shipping food to the Japanese army. They gave him food and transportation through Manchuria, and here he was—home.

"I was ashamed to come back like this—ragged and penniless," he explained. "So I waited until dark. Have the police come looking for me?"

"No, not really. But Father Yang says they are keeping an

eye on us. You must be careful. Please! Don't do anything foolish."

Her husband changed the subject. "How are the children? And my parents?"

"Everyone is fine."

"And the little one? Was it . . . was it a boy?" He seemed reluctant to hear the answer.

Soon-yul cringed. "I'm sorry, Sihwal . . . very sorry." Tears returned to her eyes. "I . . . I couldn't bring myself to give her away."

When Sihwal held their baby in his arms for the first time, a smile wreathed his face. This winsome infant had captured her father's heart. "I'm glad you kept her," he conceded to his wife. "She's so tiny and such a pretty little thing. What is her name?"

"We call her Golji, the Last One."

Her husband shook his head and answered emphatically. "No! That will never do! We must think of something special, something as pretty as she." He studied their daughter's tiny face. It was round and framed with an abundance of black hair, dominated by a pair of dark, sparkling eyes that already seemed to have unanswered questions in their depths. Suddenly Sihwal smiled. "I know! We'll name her Chung Syn, Bright Promise." With his free arm, he encircled his wife's shoulders. "May our little one's future be as bright as her smile."

CHAPTER 2

Childhood Memories

With a smile of amusement and sometimes a touch of sadness, I remember myself as a child—Chung Syn Yang, a sensitive, eager-eyed little girl looking forward to the future with faith, expectancy, and an exuberant love for life. My memories of the days when I could see God's beautiful creations are indeed precious!

After father's return from Russia the House of Yang was reunited. We were poor, but proud, and as happy as most Korean families under the occupation—until a sudden illness gripped my middle sister. Weakened by malnutrition, she died within days. Father, knowing how many times we had gone hungry during his frequent absences, blamed himself. Mother's eagerness to leave the cottage by the chapel also increased his feelings of guilt.

"Soon-yul," he began one evening after an unsuccessful search for work, "would you like to move back to our ancestral village?"

At first mother seemed uncertain. "Where you are wanted by the police?" she asked.

Father shrugged his shoulders. "There is nothing for us here," he reminded her. "Do you remember that old, secluded house on the mountainside near Song-wha? It's rundown, but the owner says we can farm the land on shares."

"Really?" mother enthused. "Maybe I could make curtains for the windows and . . ." Suddenly she stopped. "What about your parents?"

"We'll take them with us," father answered. "They are eager to go."

Mother's enthusiasm disappeared. "Whatever you say," she mumbled.

Father understood the conflict between his wife and parents. The elder Yangs had never forgiven mother for not producing a son. Gently father encircled mother's slender shoulders with his arms. "Be patient, my dear. Someday we will have a son to carry on the family name."

And so we moved! Our new home hadn't been lived in for years, but it became quite cozy after father plastered the inside walls with mud and mother covered them with newspapers. The *ondul* floors had clay flues running underneath. This ancient, forced-air heating system circulated heat from the kitchen stove and kept us warm during the winter. We were all very grateful for such a comfortable home.

Here in the hills away from the prying eyes of military police, my parents hoped for a fresh start. Together they worked long hours to make the neglected land productive. Mother even planted and cultivated when she was heavy with child.

Although it has been many years since I have actually *seen* them, the familiar scenes of my childhood—Korean blue skies, lush green meadows, and pink cherry blossoms—remain vivid in my memory. I shall never forget the titillating sight of majestic mountains rising out of the clouds with lofty peaks frosted in white, or the wonder of watching leafy green forests turn crimson and gold in the *ipchu* season. To this day I cherish the memory of those six colorful, carefree years . . . before darkness closed me in.

Father was a good man. So were his intentions, and I loved him very much. He and Sunbi, who had been my closest companion since birth, were the only ones who called me Chung Syn—instead of the detested Golji. I'm sure *ah burgi* (father) loved me, because he often brought a special treat from market, a piece of hard candy or a delicious persimmon that was ripe and ready to eat. On the nights he returned late, I stayed awake until I heard his footsteps outside. Eager for attention I would jump up from my mattress and run to the door. *Ah burgi's* arms felt so strong and warm around me!

Uh muh nee (mother) was more reserved. She seldom showed affection—especially for me. Even after a healthy, robust boy was born to the House of Yang, mother took her frustrations out on me. "Golji, can't you do anything right?" she would storm. I grew accustomed to being the last served at the table and the first blamed for trouble.

Everyone adored and pampered Choon; the boy could do no wrong. He was a cute little fellow with big black eyes and chubby cheeks. He was also full of mischief and smart enough to take advantage of the position he held in our family. Each time he turned on the tears, grandfather turned on me.

"Golji, you're a trouble maker! Why must you tease your brother?" he would shout. "Why must you be such a naughty child?" I learned to duck and run for cover, for his scoldings were followed by a glancing blow. Sunbi or father were my refuge.

In spite of our childish spats, Choon and I were the best of friends. I taught him to climb the trees in our orchard. Sometimes when the others were working in the rice paddies, we went along and chased butterflies through fields bright with wildflowers.

Choon and I owned no toys, but we did possess vivid imaginations. What adventures one didn't think of, the other did. Mother warned us not to wander too far from home, but sometimes we forgot and went scampering through the hills. We never forgot, however, to circle the village cemetery at a safe distance, since some of our neighbors practiced shamanism. They worshiped departed ancestors, and it was *spooky* to watch them as they chanted over fresh burial mounds. My brother and I were far more scared of predatory ghosts than we were of wild animals!

I also liked to visit a little Christian church in our village. People who went there seemed so happy. I enjoyed standing outside, listening to their songs about God; but since neighborhood girls often goaded me for wearing ragged clothes, I was too shy to join them. Eventually the Bible school teacher coaxed me inside, and I was spellbound by her wonderful stories.

One day this beautiful woman said something that changed my life. "Did you know, Chung Syn, that God created the world? He made animals, trees, the mountains . . . and all kinds of beautiful things for us to enjoy. Do you know why?" I shook my head, all the while watching her smiling face. "He loves us!" she exclaimed. "And we are all very, very special in His sight."

Then she handed me a picture of Jesus kneeling on the ground, arms outstretched. Gathered around Him were many children. She read aloud the verse of Scripture printed at the bottom of the page: "Let the little children come to me and do not hinder them, for the kingdom of God belongs to such as these." Later the storylady asked me to repeat those words after her and urged me to memorize them by the following Sunday.

Clutching the colorful card in my hands, I rushed home to share the good news with Sunbi. "Guess what I learned today? God created us, and He loves little children. Even me!"

After that I didn't feel like a "worthless daughter," unloved and unwanted. God thought I was special! My Bible teacher said so! Soon I had a prized collection of Bible pictures, each one a reward for memorizing—word perfect—the past week's verse.

Only Sunbi knew how much I wanted pretty clothes to wear on Sunday. One day she surprised me by saying, "You'd like a pink coat more than anything, wouldn't you?" I nodded vigorously. "Then you shall have it!"

Impulsively she took a length of neatly folded material from the treasures tucked away for her trousseau. Carefully she cut a pattern. Then, with needle, thread, and lots of love, my sister made a beautiful jacket. I had never owned anything so frivolous or lovely. For that matter, neither had Sunbi. No doubt she surmised then, although I was quite unaware, that this would be her last gift to me before leaving home.

When mother came in and saw the result of Sunbi's unselfishness, she turned livid with anger. "You took that material out of your dowry chest, didn't you?" she screamed. "Why? Tell me why you did it!" Sunbi's silence infuriated her even further. "Don't you know how long I saved to buy that for you?" By now she was in tears. "Tell me, young lady, how will you replace it? Everyone knows you can't be married without a dowry!"

Sunbi stared at the floor and made no response. Again she had taken my blame. Because I couldn't bear the thought of losing her, I deliberately dismissed from my mind Sunbi's impending marriage. After all, she had been betrothed for years. Most Korean girls were. Even I was promised, but to a six-year-old, a marriage contract meant little.

Mother warned me to wear the pink coat only on Sundays—to save it for "good." I had every intention of obeying her, but after my parents left for work the next morning, I decided to try it on. The coat was warm, soft, and beautiful. Certainly mother wouldn't mind if I showed it to a few of my friends.

Choon threatened to tattle. Even that didn't stop me. I poked my head through the door to make sure Sunbi and mama were gone. The old family dog snoozed in the sunshine. No one else was in sight, so I cautiously stepped outside. Soon the admiring glances of other girls made me forget my good intentions. Caution was thrown to the winds, and I joined them in play. Before long, careful as I tried to be, the sleeve of my precious new coat caught on a tree limb and ripped. Expecting mother to give me a whipping, I hid in the orchard until long past dark. When I finally did sneak in, scared and chilled to the core, mama shouted, "Where have you been, Golji? Everyone has been searching for you. Now see what you've done. Your new coat is ruined." Indeed, it was a sad looking sight, dirty and wrinkled. "You cause me nothing but trouble, young lady," mother continued. "Go to bed! You don't deserve any supper."

Still shivering from the cold, I crept to my mat, pulled the quilts over my head, and cried myself to sleep. Next morning my head throbbed. I felt a strange, stinging sensation behind my eyes. Rubbing them didn't help. Everything in the room looked fuzzy, and the furniture floated in space. Through parched lips, I tried to call Sunbi. No words came. All I could manage was a whimper.

Instantly Sunbi came to kneel on the clay floor, her cool, calloused hand stroking my forehead. I tried to focus my eyes on her face, but it floated behind an obscure veil. Everything spun in crazy circles.

"Mother, come quick. Chung Syn is burning with fever."

"If only your father were home," mama moaned, sinking to her knees beside Sunbi. "Wouldn't you know Golji would get sick while he's away? I hope she doesn't die before he returns!" Her frightening words were the last I heard before drifting into unconsciousness.

I later learned that neighbors came, bearing advice and home remedies. Sunbi tried everything, but nothing helped. I drifted about in semi-conscious delirium. Eventually the father of Chill-sun (the boy to whom I was promised) came to break the engagement. He shook his head and mumbled, "Poor child will never make it."

Time crept by . . . Days? Weeks? I'm not sure how long I drifted in and out of the shadows. Eventually father did return and took me to Song-wha, where I was examined by the local physician.

"I'm going to be honest with you, Mr. Yang," the doctor said. "If she does survive, Chung Syn will be blind." I heard those ominous words, but they didn't register in my befuddled brain until the two bottles of vile-tasting medicine father spooned into my mouth started to take effect.

As if by magic (or was it a miracle?), my soaring temperature dropped. Strength but not sight returned. At first I could discern dim images—shadows interspersed with flickering splotches of light. Then total darkness fell. The majestic mountains, shiny blackbirds in our barley field, pretty pink blossoms that poked their faces through our lattice fence—they all were gone.

I desperately tried to push away the veil that separated me from the sights and people I loved.

"Sunbi, where are you?" I cried, reaching out for her. "Please don't leave me. I'm afraid!"

Sister gathered me into her arms. "I'm right here, honey," she crooned. "Don't you cry." I felt her cheeks, wet with tears. Frantically I flung my arms around her neck and hung on tight.

"Why don't we go outside?" she suggested. "It's been a long time since you've sat in the sunshine."

Sunbi was right; it had been much too long. She carried me
into the yard, and we sat close to each other on a fallen stump.
How many times I had balanced myself on that same log. I
felt of the bark and filled my lungs with fresh air. A breeze
caressed my face. Upset though I was, the sunshine's warmth
refreshed me. The sounds and smells of nature seemed to heal
like a balm.

Somewhere in the yard our old red rooster crowed. "Listen
to that, Sunbi. I'll bet he's preening his feathers. Right?"

"Yes, he's strutting about, spreading his tailfeathers for his
hens to admire."

Suddenly the truth dawned: I would never again see these
familiar scenes. The thought was frightening. "My Bible
teacher was wrong, Sunbi," I sobbed. "God is not good! He is
mean . . . wicked!"

She laid a finger over my lips. "Sh-h-h. Don't say such
things."

"But it's true! And you know it! If God loves me, why did
He take away my eyes?"

Sunbi was thoughtful for a long moment. "I'm not sure,
Chung Syn. I don't have all the answers. But there must be a
good reason." Neither of us knew then that *all* things do work
together for good for those who love the Lord and are called
according to His predestination and purpose. Someday we
would both realize that God makes no mistakes. Any physical
handicap can be used for His glory—if we choose to live for
Him.

For weeks I fluctuated between childish hope and utter
despair. Healing and strength came slowly. Day after day I sat
in darkness or groped about the house in confusion—hiding
from the curious eyes of neighbors, yet dreading to be left
alone. Sunbi tried to stay home as long as possible, but the day
came when she had to return to the fields.

"Father needs me to help boll the cotton today," she

announced one morning. "And what do you think I made for your lunch? *Kimchi* and rice! Here, let me show you where to find it." Sunbi carefully guided my fingers over the familiar objects in our kitchen, cautioning me about walking too close to the stove. "And be careful. Don't cut yourself on the sharp knives." With those words of warning she walked out the door.

Choon and I had often watched fledglings try their wings for the first time. At that moment I felt as uncertain of myself as one of those baby blackbirds being nudged from the nest by its mother. Sunbi, realizing that sooner or later I would have to learn to fly alone, had wisely forced me to make my solo flight.

CHAPTER 3

New-found Faith

The Japanese occupation was difficult for father, a lovable but restless man who chafed under the yoke of suppression. He seemed to search endlessly for the rainbow's gold, on several occasions leaving mother to care for our family alone while he sought a better way of life.

Mother, after working long hours in the rice paddies, returned home at night to care for babies, mend clothes, and keep house. Despite her efforts we had scarcely enough money to provide necessities, much less luxuries. Gradually hardships and the added burden of a blind daughter crushed her spirit, and she became embittered. My presence was a continual reminder of things she wanted to forget! No doubt mother suffered as much humiliation as I when friends referred to my blindness as a curse, or when children snickered when I stumbled.

Nothing is more shattering to a child than rejection. I felt unloved, unwanted, worthless. Such insecurity and lack of understanding made my transition into a world of darkness far more difficult than it might have been. Occasionally father

showed moments of compassion, but only Sunbi really
understood my craving for love.

Our local lay pastor heard about the misfortune that had
befallen the House of Yang and dropped by one afternoon
while my parents were away. He found me in tears. "Why are
you crying, Chung Syn? You are such a special little girl, and
God loves you."

"Then why did He make me blind?"

"Some things we don't understand . . . not yet. But God has
a plan for each of us."

His answer didn't satisfy me. "But I don't like to be blind!
I'm lonesome . . . and afraid of the dark."

"There is no need to be afraid. Or lonely either," he said,
"for you and I have a heavenly Father."

"A heavenly Father?" I asked, puzzled by this new term.

"Yes, my dear, *God* is also our Father. Even though we
can't see Him, He is always near. You can talk to Him when
you are lonely, just like you do to your own *ah burgi*." He went
on to explain that God is only a prayer away and that we can
call on Him for help during times of trouble.

Although this wise, humble layman was not educated, he
knew and understood the Word of God. He also knew how to
comfort the heart of a frightened, bewildered child. Pastor Lee
knelt beside me and with simple, sincere words taught me to
pray. Through him I learned the meaning of Christian love.

Several days later he returned, this time to tell my parents
that a well-known evangelist was conducting a series of
meetings in the small town of Chungyung. I listened from the
kitchen while they talked.

"Why don't you take your daughter to see Rev. Kim and
ask him to pray for her?"

"Do you think he would?" father asked.

"I understand there have been some miraculous healings,"
Pastor Lee answered.

Father, hoping for a miracle, borrowed an ox cart. He and mother took me to the neighboring village that following day. After the evening service Rev. Kim gave an altar call, and the three of us went forward. Father told the famous evangelist that I was blind and asked him to pray for my sight. With one hand on my head, the other placed over my eyes, he began. We all waited expectantly. As his voice droned on and on my heart beat faster and faster.

Rev. Kim closed with the words, "May Thy will be done," then told me to open my eyes. I did, one at a time, but God had not seen fit to perform a miracle.

Father, unable to accept the Lord's will, lashed out in bitterness and anger. "Miracles? Bah! God has no mercy. Nothing has changed! Our daughter is still blind." At one time father had claimed to be a Christian, had even attended a Bible college during his youth, but after this service he refused to believe or attend church. It took many years and lots of hard knocks before my father returned to the Lord.

I had always been a friendly, outgoing child, but during my adjustment to blindness I became withdrawn and frightened of the unknown, shrinking from the sound of strange voices. I was tormented by what felt like crawling insects behind my eyes. No one explained to me then (perhaps my parents didn't even know) that damaged nerves heal slowly. Without proper medical attention my eye sockets were inflamed and extremely sensitive for many months.

Equally frustrating was the feeling that an opaque curtain or film of some sort hung over my eyes. Whatever it was blocked my sight, and I felt impelled to remove it by shaking my head, blinking, and rubbing until my eyelids were sore. Nothing helped. Finally, out of sheer desperation, I picked at the pupils and scratched with my fingernails, causing painful and irreversible damage.

Sunbi was aghast after discovering what I had done. Not

knowing how else to help, she held a damp cloth over my eyelids until the bleeding stopped. "Don't cry, little one," she soothed. "Soon the hurt will go away."

Soon Sunbi would go away also—without warning and without telling me good-by!

On a cool, crisp morning I sensed excitement in the air. Visitors and relatives were gathering but I knew it was too early for Christmas. Since mother was busy greeting guests and had been impatient with me all morning, I went in search of father who was on our front porch with a group of neighborhood men.

"What's happening?" I whispered, trying not to attract attention.

"Don't you know?" father asked. "This is Sunbi's wedding day. Your sister is about to be married." I knew that Sunbi was betrothed but hadn't given the reality of marriage much thought. Nor did I understand what such a union involved.

Mother gave Choon and me a handful of water chestnuts and sent us outside to eat them. "Stay on the porch . . . and Golji, don't get your dress dirty," she warned.

After the wedding ceremony, when the guests started leaving, Sunbi came outside. "I have a surprise for you, Chung Syn. Hold out your hands." Gently she closed my fingers around two ripe persimmons. "Come sit on my lap, little one, and let me hold you close." Careful not to squash the treat she had brought, I snuggled contentedly in my sister's arms and went to sleep as she crooned a lullaby. When I wakened sometime later Sunbi had gone, and mother's sister was sitting beside me.

"Where is Sunbi?" I asked.

"She has gone away," my aunt answered, "to live with her new husband."

"No! Sister wouldn't leave without saying good-by! You aren't telling me the truth!" She tried to console and control me, but nothing my aunt did or said eased the hurt inside. In vain I fought her restraining hands and tried to follow Sunbi. Why? Why had she deserted me? How could I get along without the one who had mothered me since the day of my birth? My childish mind didn't then understand that sister had sung me to sleep because she couldn't face a tearful good-by.

Every morning for two weeks I groped my way up the hill and kept a lonely vigil by the wayside, hoping and praying that Sunbi would come home. When she did it was only for a brief visit, for now sister had a husband . . . and a new home.

Fortunately broken hearts mend, and with the resiliency of youth I gradually adjusted to blindness. No doubt Sunbi's marriage forced me to mature and find ways of taking care of myself. I learned to play and laugh again, until sometimes Choon seemed to forget that I couldn't see. We both liked to romp with Noo-rung, the family dog. Once again I joined Choon in climbing mulberry trees, and together we picked wildflowers in the meadow. Sometimes, when I stumbled and skinned my shins or knees, mother scolded me for getting my clothes dirty, but not even that slowed me down.

When I was eight, Choon became suddenly and seriously ill with an undiagnosed illness. Since he and I shared the same pallet, four days later I suffered from the same symptoms. Our temperatures soared out of control, and nothing the country doctor prescribed brought them down. In the past Choon had been robust and healthy. Now my parents were frantic over the possibility of losing their only son.

Early one morning I wakened after a restless and feverish night. The room seemed strangely silent. Unable to hear Choon laboring for breath, I called out his name. He didn't answer. I rolled over and touched his face. It felt cold and lifeless. Choon had gone to be with the Lord!

We were all heartbroken, especially Grandfather Yang. The

light of his life had gone out, and the poor old man seemed to lose his mind—weeping, wailing, and beating his chest as neighbors nailed together a crude coffin.

Mother didn't express her grief verbally but kept it all inside. I don't think she ever recovered from the sorrow of losing this child, her long-cherished dream. Because mother bitterly resented my survival and his death, she started staying away from home—often for days at a time. During her absences I longed for companionship. Yet many nights when she did come home, I crept to my pallet and cried myself to sleep because of her contempt and rejection.

Father was never unkind, just preoccupied with his own grief and the responsibility of providing for his family. I feared that he might send me away to become a fortuneteller—or worse yet, a beggar. It also made me sad to see his bitterness toward God grow after Choon's untimely death.

Noo-rung became my self-appointed guide. The old dog seemed to sense my loneliness. He guarded me closely, growling when danger loomed, barking when someone came close. How grateful I was for his faithfulness.

Without Sunbi to intercede, my next-oldest sister became a tyrant. She taunted and tormented me at every opportunity and constantly goaded me about being blind. One bitterly cold night when I was left in her care, Yoon locked me out of the house during a snowstorm. With the coming of darkness my teeth began to chatter. Fearful of freezing I blew on my hands, rubbing them together while walking in circles around the yard. Noo-rung trotted at my side, whimpering occasionally but never leaving. Soon a stray dog from the village joined us.

I tried to stay on my feet, but eventually numbness and exhaustion made me give up and lie down. Noo-rung crept closer, his warm body beside mine. Somehow, no doubt by the providence of God, the warmth of those two shaggy mongrels—snuggled close on each side—kept me alive until morning.

Grandfather's bitterness over having a blind granddaughter grew with his grief. He blamed me for Choon's death, forced me to go without meals, and, when friends came to smoke and play chess at our house, he would tell me to hide. I dreaded the times when we were alone and tried to stay out of his way.

I also feared grandfather's influence over the others. "Why don't you send Golji to a clairvoyant, Soon-yul? Let her become a fortuneteller. She's not good for anything else!" Out of filial respect father kept silent, but such threats hung over my head like ominous storm clouds.

Only once did I try to tell mother how lonely I was for Sunbi and how cruel the others were when she left. Instead of being sympathetic she shook me and shouted, "Stop sniveling, Golji. I'm sick of your complaints. Don't you think I have problems of my own?"

Poor mother! She did have her problems though I was too young then to understand why she had so much difficulty bending and doing her chores. Mother was expecting again!

Soon after another son was born to carry on the House of Yang, they laid grandfather to rest beside his ancestors in the village cemetery. My father was deeply grieved, and for his sake I *tried* to feel sad. But no tears came to my eyes. Instead a sense of relief swept over me. No more beatings! No more threats! Such joy made me feel guilty, although I suspected that mother shared these same emotions.

Three months later Grandmother Yang joined her husband.

After the mourning period was over and the time had come for my parents to return to work, father laid a calloused hand on my shoulder. "Chung Syn," he said, "I need your mother to help me with the harvest. Now that Yoon is married and your grandmother has been laid to rest, there is no one left to care for the children." As he spoke father stroked my hair. His voice sounded so weary, and starved as I was for affection his sudden show of tenderness made me feel happy and important.

"Maybe I could help, *ah burgi*. After all, I'm quite grown up now."

"Yes . . . and blind."

"But I'm strong, father. You said so yourself. I already help with the kitchen chores. I can build fires, even cook rice. Don't you remember? Last summer I learned to cut cabbage for the *kimchi* pots."

Father's arm around my shoulders tightened. "Yes *ahga* (baby), I remember. Sometimes I am surprised by the things you can do . . . and I almost forget that you can't see. But what about your little brother? He could crawl close to the fire—without you even knowing it."

"I've already thought of that. I'll carry the baby on my back, and Yu-nok can keep an eye on him while he plays."

"I don't doubt that you can, Chung Syn, but it hardly seems fair." Father turned to mother. "What do you think, Soon-yul?"

Mother expressed neither confidence in my ability nor concern over putting so much responsibility on my shoulders. All she said was, "What choice do we have?"

"We could ask your mother to come for a while."

"Nonsense! *Uh muh nee* has her own household to care for. Chung Syn can manage . . . somehow."

Little did I know that God, even then, was preparing me, teaching me independence so I could cope with all the exciting challenges that lay ahead.

CHAPTER 4

A Glimmer of Hope

One sultry summer day my parents left me home to care for the two children while they transplanted seedlings. Toward evening the baby acted hungry, and since mother still breast fed the little fellow I took him to the field where she worked.

"Black clouds are gathering," she told me after nursing the baby. "Hurry home with the children, Golji. I'll come, too, just as soon as I have finished this row." Quickly she tied the baby on my back. "Better gather some kindling on the way," she added. "I used the last this morning."

As Yu-nok and I picked up twigs along the trail it started to sprinkle. This was the monsoon season. Light sprinkles could turn into a downpour within minutes. Not wanting to be caught in a summer storm I urged my sister to hurry. Claps of thunder were starting to shake the ground beneath our feet.

"I can't tell which way we are going, Yu-nok. You'll have to help me."

"This is the right trail," she yelled above the wind. "And we are almost there." I followed the sound of her voice as she ran ahead, and just as we stepped inside rain pounded the

thatched roof. Thankful for dry kindling I built a fire and put
a pot of rice on the stove to boil, finishing just as someone
knocked at the front door. Noo-rung growled, and Yu-nok
peeked through the window.

"Can you see who's there?" I asked.

"It's a man. I've never seen him before."

Quickly I opened the door "Hello," a stranger greeted.
"May I come in?"

"Of course. Please do."

"Thank you, young lady," the friendly voice responded. "I
am soaked to the skin." He slipped out of his shoes and left
them by the door. "Your floor is warm to my feet. May I take
shelter here until the storm passes?"

"Come closer to the stove, sir. You are welcome to stay as
long as you like."

"My name is Ung-Ku Choe," he told me as I brewed a pot
of tea. "I was on my way to Pyongyang when the storm broke.
I must have gotten lost."

Immediately I liked Mr. Choe and sensed something
different about him. He had called me young lady and had
made no reference to my blindness. Had he not noticed?

Later father and our guest talked while mother and I
listened from the kitchen. When Mr. Choe said he was a
secretary and *sun seng nim* (teacher) at Chung-Jin School for
the Blind, my curiosity got out of hand. *What,* I wondered, *is a
blind school?*

"We teach children to read and write *Hangul* (the Korean
alphabet), as well as Japanese," he explained to father.

"How can this be if your students are blind?"

"We use the Braille system. With a stylus raised dots are
produced on paper. These dots are grouped together and
represent letters of the alphabet. Our students are taught to
feel them with their fingertips."

"Do you mean people actually read with their hands?"

"Exactly, and it is amazing how fast the children catch on. Mr. Yang, would you be interested in enrolling Chung Syn?"

Father evaded the question. "Maybe later."

Our guest was persistent. "Why not now, sir?"

"Pyongyang is a long way from home. Besides, a blind, country girl doesn't need schooling."

Mr. Choe's candid reply came straight to the point. "Without an education, Mr. Yang, your daughter will live in a world of darkness for the rest of her life. If Chung Syn learns to read she will see things through the eyes of others." He paused. "Perhaps the old Chinese proverb says it best: 'If you are planning for a year, plant rice. If you are planning for a decade, plant trees. But if you are planning for a lifetime, educate a child.'" Mr. Choe's words gave me new hope. "Think it over, sir," he continued. "Can you, in good conscience, deprive your daughter of an education?"

Neither man spoke for several seconds and the silence seemed to stretch into infinity. "We can't afford it," father finally mumbled.

"I see. If a partial scholarship could be arranged, would you reconsider?"

"Well . . . maybe." As indefinite as father's answer was, my mind bubbled with the possibility of going away to school. Would the other girls accept someone without money or pretty clothes? Would they all be rich?

Mr. Choe made a promise that within ten days he would let us know the school board's decision. The minute our guest was gone mother started fuming. "Don't fill this girl's head with nonsense, Sihwal. We don't have money to send her to school, and you know it. Besides, she's needed here. Who will take care of the children?"

"We'll find a way," father answered mechanically. "Somehow."

Not even mother's pessimistic remarks could dampen my

enthusiasm or dash my daydreams, for I felt confident that Mr. Choe's coming had not been accidental. So, if the scholarship were to be granted, I had to learn how to do everything for myself—and there was no time to waste!

First came my hair. Usually my long locks just blew with the breeze, but one morning mother braided them for church. Knowing she would be furious if I told her my plans, I waited until mother stepped outside, then ran my fingers over the long smooth braids. I tried to visualize how the locks were intertwined and discovered, after loosening the ribbons, that each queue had three strands. It seemed simple. But weaving the locks back in position wasn't as easy as taking them apart!

I didn't hear mother enter the room until she shouted, "Golji! What in heaven's name are you doing? I fixed your hair and now it's a mess!" she stormed, yanking my hair as she rebraided it. Why try to explain? Mother seldom listened to me anyway, especially when she was angry. Later I tried again and within a short time had conquered hurdle number one. Although my braids were a trifle lopsided at first, I had confidence that fixing my hair would be simple in the future.

Next I tackled the laundry. Washing a skirt and blouse presented no problems, but laundering a Korean coat was challenging. First it had to be taken apart, the lining and cotton batting carefully removed, then stitched back in place when the garment was dry and the wrinkles had been pounded out with a board.

All went well until I came to the last step. I remembered watching mother and Sunbi sew. It had seemed so easy for them. But I struggled for one hour trying to thread a single needle. Either the eye was too small or the thread too thick. I never did get the coat back together. When mother discovered my efforts, she yelled. "Golji, this coat isn't dirty. I just washed it. Why did you rip out the lining?"

"Because I wanted to wash it myself." Mother scolded as

she stitched the garment back together, but her words went unheeded. My mind was on other things. There *had* to be a way of threading those needles, and I intended to find it!

Ten days passed. Then twenty. Father tried to prepare me for disappointment, but I refused to give up hope. One of my main goals in life was to make him proud of me and to hear mother say, "Chung Syn, you are a good daughter. I love you very much." Why did she dislike me? Why was she ashamed of having a blind daughter? I finally confided in Pastor Lee.

"You really want to attend school, don't you Chung Syn?" he asked. I nodded. "Then pray . . . and ask *God* to give you that scholarship."

"I already have."

He patted my hand. "Then be patient. Your answer is on its way."

The next day a letter arrived. Father slit the slender envelope and read its message aloud.

Dear Mr. Yang,

   I am pleased to inform you that your daughter has been awarded a scholarship to attend Chung-Jin School for the Blind. It will cover half of all her expenses—tuition, books, and dormitory fees. We shall expect you to pay the rest. Classes are ready to start. I do hope Chung Syn will be happy here.

                                        By God's grace,
                                        Ung-Ku Choe

"Isn't it wonderful, father? God answered my prayers. Pastor Lee said He would."

"Maybe you are right, Chung Syn. I hope so."

"How soon can we leave? Tomorrow morning?" Father sat in silence, undoubtedly wondering how he would raise his share of the money. Not until years later did I realize the sacrifices he made.

Packing was not a problem; I had so few possessions. Father

bought me a new pair of stockings. Mother washed and mended my *ibul* (quilt), then tucked a change of underclothes, one skirt, and two blouses inside the roll. At that time I had no fears or second thoughts about leaving home. Today I realize that three things were in my favor—youth, faith, and lots of determination.

Pastor Lee came to say good-by. "You have a bright future ahead of you, Chung Syn, but it's a big world out there—with much to learn. As long as you walk with the Lord, He will meet your needs." Those were his parting and prophetic words.

On the day of our departure I found Noo-rung, sunning himself on the front porch. My canine friend seemed to sense that I was leaving. He barked and nuzzled a wet nose into the palm of my hand, as though encouraging me to stroke his shaggy head. Impulsively I knelt and put both arms around the old dog's neck. Noo-rung, delighted over all the attention, wagged his tail wildly and licked my face.

"Take care of the children while I'm gone, Noo-rung. And thanks for saving my life. I won't forget you, ever!"

Relatives and neighbors gathered to say farewell and warn me about all the dangers that lurked in the big city. Some expressed sadness. Others said nothing. One farmer's wife summarized the sentiments of everyone present. "Sihwal, this poor child would be better off to stay here and become a *mudang* (female exorcist of evil spirits). How can a blind girl make it all alone in the city?"

I resolved to show her!

My maternal grandmother wept. "Why are you sending Golji away to school, Soon-yul? Heaven only knows what will happen to her in Pyongyang."

Mother didn't answer. She was torn between relief and regret—relief to have the burdensome care of a blind daughter lifted from her shoulders, regret over losing her baby sitter.

Only father and Sunbi would really miss me. They alone had confidence that I could amount to something, and I vowed not to let them down.

At the bus stop the two children did all the chattering. Everyone else seemed strangely silent. Yu-nok climbed on my lap and flung her chubby little arms around my neck, not understanding why *uhn-nee* (big sister) was going away. Teuk-Choon vied for attention by pulling my braids.

Finally Sunbi announced the coming of our bus. She kissed me and straightened my collar. "I will miss you, little sister. Be careful . . . and write real soon." There was a catch in her voice.

I barely had time to hug everyone before boarding the bus that took me into a whole new world full of unbelievable challenges. As we rumbled along the dusty roads I slipped my hand into father's. It was such fun to share this new experience with my beloved *ah burgi*.

To this very day reminiscing makes me chuckle. What an eager, naive child I was, sitting there on the bouncing bus with a picnic lunch of freshly cooked sweet potatoes on my lap and a small bundle of belongings at my feet. Can it possibly be that half-a-century has since passed?

CHAPTER 5

School Daze

While our bus clattered over muddy country trails, father described the scenery in detail. My head was in a whirl, trying to take it all in.

"You will like Pyongyang, Chung Syn. It is an exciting city. It may seem a little confusing at first, but you will get used to it." A bit later he said, "Here is where I attended Bible school. . . . Over that hill is where my brother lives. Wish we had time to stop and say hello."

"You have been everywhere, haven't you, *ah burgi?*" I asked with wonder.

Father laughed. It was good to hear him so carefree and relaxed. "No, *ahga,*" he answered, squeezing my hand. "I haven't been everywhere . . . not quite."

Later that day we boarded a train. The wheels of that speeding locomotive could scarcely keep pace with my questions. A whole new world was passing before me. I didn't want to miss a thing.

Toward dusk we rumbled across the Tae-dong Bridge, our passenger car lurching as though it would leave the tracks.

Suddenly the conductor bellowed, "Pyongyang! Pyongyang! Everybody off."

"This is the end of the line," father announced. "We're here." When the train came to a screeching stop he picked up my parcel and guided me down the steps. Once my foot slipped, and his grip tightened.

Activity surrounded us on all sides. I heard exciting noises—the hustle and bustle of people on the move, train whistles, shouting porters, and banging luggage. It all blended into a fascinating cacophony of pleasing sounds.

Being a part of the unseen confusion made me feel as though I had suddenly emerged from a cocoon—like the silkworms back home. Was this really me, Chung Syn Yang, about to become a part of city life?

Father asked a porter for directions, and in another few minutes we were standing before the door of Chung-Jin School for the Blind. A night watchman answered our knock and invited us in. When I was properly introduced and registered, father left to find lodging for the night, promising to return the next day.

Alone for the first time, doubts assailed me, and I felt a bit deflated. *What now? Would the other students accept me? Could I make friends and adjust to this new way of life?* I didn't have long to wonder.

Soon the school secretary interrupted my thoughts, "Chung Syn, this is Soon-ja, one of our older students. She will help you find a bed for the night. Tomorrow you will receive your permanent assignment."

"Thank you," I stammered. "Thank you very much."

Soon-ja took my arm and guided me down the hall. "In no time at all every square inch of this place will be as familiar as your face."

"Are you . . . are you blind, too?" I asked.

"Yes, all the students who live here are blind. But we attend classes on the same campus as sighted students. Tonight you may sleep in my room. We have an empty bed."

The instant we stepped through the door her roommates surrounded us, bombarding me with questions about my home and family.

"How many brothers and sisters do you have?" one asked.

"There were eight of us. Only five are still living."

"Are any of the others blind?"

"No, I am the only one."

"That's good. My brother and sister are blind, too. Father says it runs in our family."

"Do you miss your mother?" one of the younger girls inquired.

"No, not really." Why tell them that mother was glad to be rid of me? They wouldn't understand.

"I was so lonely at first that I cried for two weeks. But it's fun living here now. Everyone is so nice! You'll like it too, Chung Syn. Just wait and see."

As soon as their curiosity about my family was satisfied, exploring hands started to feel of my face and shoulders. I backed away.

"Don't be embarrassed, Chung Syn," the dorm director said. "Everyone wants to know what you look like," she explained. "Here at the school students *see* with their hands."

After touching me lightly with her fingertips one girl exclaimed, "You are the smallest girl here. I'll be your big sister."

Soon-ja led me to a mattress on stilts. "This is your bed," she announced. "I'll help you spread the blankets."

"This is a . . . *bed*? Do you ever fall off?"

Soon-ja laughed. "Don't worry. You'll get used to it, just as the rest of us did." Frankly I would have been much more comfortable sleeping in a cozy *ibul* if it were spread on the warm *ondul* floor back home.

Long after the others had gone to sleep I lay on my strange new bed and reviewed the day. Gratitude filled my heart. Already I felt a part of these new surroundings and thanked God for bringing me to the blind school.

Reveille bell rang at six every morning. That first day I was awake and waiting. Immediately the dormitory started to buzz with chattering voices—the carefree voices of girls who felt loved and secure. Soon-ja shared her wash basin with me, and another pair of willing hands helped to fasten my blouse buttons.

I shall never forget the menu that day. How could I? I ate the same thing for five years. For breakfast we were served millet. Too keyed-up to eat, I passed my portion to the girl sitting beside me.

"Don't you like it?" she asked.

"I'm not hungry," I whispered back. She devoured both servings, and I learned my first lesson: Students who failed to clean up their plates one meal ate leftovers—or nothing—the next. I got no lunch that first day!

Classes started right after chapel, and we walked the short distance to the rhythmic accompaniment of tapping white canes. Since I was unaccustomed to the surroundings, big sister led me. Our school shared playground facilities with an adjoining school for sighted students. Those in charge felt the handicapped needed to commingle and learn how to cope in an unprotected environment.

When we were halfway across the yard, a sighted student yelled, "Watch out, *chambong*. There's a ditch ahead." The remark was followed by loud guffaws.

"Don't pay any attention to him, Chung Syn. There's nothing in the way. He's just a bully, poking fun of us because we can't see." *Chambong,* she explained, was a derogatory term used for the blind.

There were a few hecklers in the public school, but everyone

else was kind and helpful. I liked my teacher. Miss Chun, also
blind, had a soft voice and sensitive spirit. I felt an affinity for
her immediately.

Mornings we attended classes in the basics: Braille, history,
and the three R's. During afternoon sessions we learned
sewing skills, knitting, and massage.

When father returned that evening he brought me a black
uniform skirt, a wash basin, and a large box of apples to share
with the girls in my dorm. He was always thoughtful and
generous.

"Study hard, Chung Syn," he told me. "Obey your teachers
. . . and write to us." He sounded sad. Would he miss me?

"Thank you, *ah burgi,* for everything. Please tell the children
I love them." Father squeezed my hand, then left. As his
footsteps echoed down the hall I felt a tinge of loneliness—
which quickly passed.

My mind was like a thirsty sponge—quick to absorb.
Studying was not a bore, but a joy. There simply weren't
enough hours between classes to learn what I wanted to know.
Several times I was chastised by the dorm director for
studying after the lights-out bell. But, who needed lights to
study? Long after the others were asleep I fingered my Braille
reader under the covers. Because of the Japanese occupation,
all students were required to study two languages. In record
time I had mastered both alphabets, as well as Braille.

My teacher was amazed by my rapid progress, and, hungry
as I was for approval, her encouragement spurred me on. It
was Miss Chun's compliments, a desire to excel, and my first
savory taste of success that gave me a ravenous appetite for
learning. While my roommates engaged in girlish chitchat, I
lost myself in a wonderful world of books. The school
principal, confident that I could compete with sighted
students, soon advanced me to the third grade.

When winter winds started to whistle across campus, all of

us shivered from the cold. The other girls wore head scarves and gloves. I had neither and knew that my only coat was undoubtedly dirty from constant use. With grim determination I decided to tackle the task that had defeated me once before. After dismantling my coat I scrubbed, starched, and hung it to dry, intending to stitch the lining back after my "roomies" were asleep. This, I reasoned, would give me more study time.

I had the maid thread five needles in advance, and carefully laid them in a row. Although my sewing skills had increased since last time, each thread either tangled, broke, or eventually slipped out of the eye. I tried to rethread each needle. My efforts were futile. What now? I needed that coat by morning!

Frustrated about not being able to see, I wakened the maid to ask for help. She was furious! "Go back to bed or I'll report you to the principal . . . first thing in the morning."

I returned to my room in tears—but not defeated. It was then that Pastor Lee's words came back to me: "God will not forsake you. When you have problems, when things go wrong, talk it over with Him."

Kneeling beside my cot, I whispered a simple prayer. "Dear God, you know I can't see. Please . . . please help me find a way to thread those needles."

Immediately, as though by divine inspiration, the solution came to me. Softly I slipped down the hall and pulled several of the thinnest straws out of our old dorm broom. Back in my room I tried to slip one through the unseen eye of the needle. The first was too thick. So was the second. But I finally found a wisp that would pass through the needle's eye with little effort. Next I tried strands of hair. That wasn't as easy, but persistence did pay off. Finally, and with trembling fingers, I was ready to work with the elusive thread.

What a letdown! The cotton strand was limp,

unmanageable. For hours, it seemed, I struggled without one shred of encouragement. Yet I refused to give up. Toward morning, when it appeared that my efforts were in vain and success had evaded me for the second time, victory came!

Thinking the needle had threaded itself by accident, I tried again . . . and again. Each time the needle and thread responded to my sensitive fingertips in the same miraculous way. I wanted to shout with joy! Waken the whole dorm! Instead I kept practicing until reveille. By then I could thread the needles every time.

I demonstrated my expertise to the dorm director, who excitedly paraded me before the principal.

Miss Chun was also full of congratulations. "You have not only broken a barrier for the blind, but you've also learned a valuable lesson. Some tasks are harder than others, but with determination and God's help, nothing is impossible."

CHAPTER 6

A Hard Lesson

School life was all that I had dreamed it would be—and more! I looked forward to each day and dreaded hearing the lights-out bell at night. It was an unwelcome intruder. Fearful that my time at Chung-Jin might be cut short, I felt compelled to cram everything possible into each twenty-four hours. Even our monotonous diet of millet, cabbage, and bean-paste soup couldn't dull my appetite for learning!

At home, I had been lonely. In the dorm, there was almost too much company, too little time for study. My family had never been able to understand the frustrations of being blind. Nor did they realize the anguish their unkind ridicule caused. Here, blindness was a common denominator, a cohesive bond. Everyone understood!

The teachers, some sightless themselves, were empathetic. They appreciated our needs and taught us to meet them independently, with a minimum of assistance. We were encouraged to do things for ourselves. Each girl was given a rotating assignment, some in housekeeping, others in the dining hall, so we would learn self-sufficiency, a necessary prerequisite for competing in a sighted world.

Being accepted as a normal person was a big boost to my self-confidence. I felt loved, worthwhile, and motivated to strive for bigger and better things.

My rapid progress surprised even the administrators, and after being the target of cruel, caustic criticism for years, words of praise were most welcome. To earn additional encores, I made up my mind to achieve academic excellence. Driven by this deep desire to excel, I often hid Braille books under the covers and sometimes studied for hours after others in the dorm were sleeping.

Occasionally I did worry about not getting enough sleep, but recklessly pushed the thought aside. After all, wasn't I young and healthy? Only the weak and sickly came down with malaria or tuberculosis.

In my new, congenial environment, unhappy memories were easy to forget, but poverty—like Mary's little lamb—had followed me to school. Father scrimped and saved to pay his half of school expenses, but I had no money for incidentals. That first winter I had only one pair of stockings. Saturdays I washed, mended, and put them on again—each time praying they would last a little longer.

Too proud to confide in anyone, I started scavenging through the trash for castoffs. If someone discarded a pair of old hose, regardless of how worn they were, I quickly retrieved them. No doubt the dorm supervisor was aware, but to protect my pride and dignity she kept silent. If my friends surmised, they were equally discrete; no one told my secret.

Most of the girls who shared our dorm were friendly and uninhibited. None seemed to resent, at least openly, the praise I received for good grades. In fact, they constantly encouraged me. Only Pong-lak remained aloof. Although I went out of my way to win her approval, she avoided me, and I sensed something smoldering beneath the surface.

One morning Kim stopped me in the hall. "Chung Syn," she called in a stage whisper. "Have you heard the news?"

"What news?"

"There's a thief in our midst!" She paused for a moment to let the startling news sink in. "At first it was pencils, then a bar of soap. Yesterday Kwang Myung lost her scarf."

"Maybe the wind blew it away," I ventured.

"You haven't heard the worst yet," Kim insisted. "Today Pong-lak's tuition money vanished."

"No! I can't believe it!" By now I was all ears.

"Until that money's found, we're all in trouble—big trouble!" Kim retorted. "Don't leave your money lying around," she cautioned. The bell rang, and we hurried in different directions.

After dinner that evening Miss Shinn sent us all back to the dining hall while she and the maid searched our rooms. As we waited in silence, each girl seemed absorbed with her own thoughts.

Finally Min whispered, "Are you scared, Chung Syn?"

"Of course not!" I retorted. "I'm innocent. Why worry?"

A short while later the others were sent back to their sleeping quarters. Only Pong-lak, and I were to remain. Why would they want to question *me*? I was more puzzled than concerned.

"Chung Syn," the dorm director began, her voice as frigid as a Siberian wind in January. "Why did you do this? I can't believe an honor student would stoop to steal from a classmate." Her words, spoken with unmistakable contempt, stung like a slap across the face.

"I'm not surprised!" Pong-lak exclaimed with relish. "Chung Syn is a thief!"

I tried to stammer something in my own defense. "But . . . but all I took were old stockings that had been thrown away."

"Stop pretending, Chung Syn. You know what I mean. The

money was found in the back pages of your reader."

"I don't understand."

"Stop pretending," she repeated. "Lying is as bad as stealing." Grasping my shoulders, she shook me soundly, as if she could shake loose the truth.

"But Miss Shinn, I didn't take Pong-lak's money. I've never stolen anything. Please believe me."

She refused to listen. "Go to your room," she snapped, "and think about what you have done!"

I ran to my room, undressed quickly, and slipped into bed. "You know I'm innocent, Lord. Please . . . please help me convince them," I repeated over and over.

Right after breakfast the principal summoned me to her office. My teacher was there also. Miss Haines, her voice filled with emotion, took my hand in hers. "Chung Syn, were you that desperate for money?" I couldn't answer. Taking my silence as an admission of guilt, she continued. "Don't you know that stealing is a sin? Unless you confess and repent, the Lord won't forgive you. Neither can we."

"But Miss Haines, I didn't do it. Please . . . please believe me." By now I was near hysterics.

"We want to believe you. But the money was found in your book. Remember?" Her voice softened. "If you confess and apologize, all will be forgiven."

Tears stung my eyes. Even Miss Haines spoke of confession and repentance as though guilt were a foregone conclusion.

"Chung Syn, you are making it difficult for everyone. Must I call your father?"

"Please don't," I pled. "Father would be furious. Give me a little time. I'm innocent. You'll see."

Miss Haines turned to my disappointed teacher. "I have no choice but to place Chung Syn on suspension. Until further notice she is not to attend classes."

Fighting to hold back my tears, I returned to the dorm,

passing chattering groups enroute. More than once I heard my friends say, "I can't believe Chung Syn is a thief!" But I was too crushed to defend myself. Let them believe what they would!

For two weeks I lived under a cloud of suspicion, studying and eating my meals in isolation. Eventually I began to doubt myself. Could I have taken the money while sleepwalking? Was I suffering from a lapse of memory? These introspective grillings always ended the same—in confusion. Only God knew how much I was hurting.

One evening I overheard the girls talking about revival meetings that were being held downtown. Both the staff and the students were scheduled to attend. I went by myself and found great comfort in Rev. Nam-Su-Chung's message. His words encouraged me, as though the future held some hope.

Later I learned that others had been similarly affected by the message—even Pong-lak. Eager to make amends, she confessed that jealousy had prompted her to plant the money in my book.

"I'm sorry, Chung Syn," she wailed. "It was all my fault."

"But . . . why did you do it?"

"I hated you . . . you make such good grades and have more friends than I do." She stopped and sniffled before adding, "I've asked the Lord to forgive me, Chung Syn. Will . . . will you forgive me, too?"

My first reaction was anger! For two weeks I had suffered unjustly because of Pong-lak's lies, but suddenly the ice around my heart melted. Impulsively I reached out and touched her hand.

"Of course, Pong-lak, I forgive you. Maybe now we can be friends."

God heard and answered my prayers in His own time and in His own way. He also taught me a lesson that I have never forgotten.

CHAPTER 7

From the Depths of Despair

"Thank goodness summer vacation will be here soon," my roommate announced in the middle of a study session. "I can hardly wait to go home." Myung-Eh walked to the open window before asking, "What are you planning to do this year, Chung Syn?"

"Nothing special. Probably what I've done for the past three summers: help the dorm maid with housecleaning."

"But you need a vacation. It's been years since you've seen your family. Why not go home for a change?"

"I can't afford the train fare. Besides, the dorm supervisor has asked me to stay and look after five orphan children this summer while she and the cook are gone."

At that moment our conversation was interrupted by the school secretary: "Chung Syn, you received mail today. Looks like a letter from your father. Shall I read it aloud?"

"Yes, please do," I responded. While listening to Miss Wong unfold a crackly sheet of rice paper I wondered if something could be wrong. Father rarely wrote—unless there was an emergency. Had there been a death in the family?

Were mother and the children well? Fear and a sudden surge of homesickness came over me as I waited.

My dear daughter,

I hope you are well and that you will not be too disappointed when you learn why I am writing. For the past two years conditions here at home have been very bad, and no longer am I able to pay for half of your tuition. We have sold our possessions, one by one, in order to meet our bills. Now there is nothing left to sell.

You have done well in school, Chung Syn, and I know how much you want to graduate with your class. Under the circumstances that will not be possible. When this semester is over I will borrow money to send for you.

I am sorry. Please forgive me for letting you down.

Your father,
Sihwal Yang

Myung-Eh started to sniffle. A lump rose to my own throat, but I was still too stunned for tears. *Did this mean that all my plans, all my hopes for the future were ending before they had hardly begun?*

Miss Wong slipped an arm around my shoulders. "Oh Chung Syn, I'm so sorry. Everyone at Chung-Jin will miss you." Her sympathy and kind words opened the floodgates. I started to cry, and she held me close.

"I *can't* go home," I sobbed. "Mother doesn't want me. And father has enough to worry about already. There has to be a way for me to support myself. I *want* to graduate . . . and make my parents proud of me."

"Have you prayed about it?" asked Miss Wong.

"Every day!"

"Then God will help you find a way," she assured me, closing my fingers around several silver coins and a crumpled bill. "This money is yours. In all the excitement I almost forgot to give it to you. We not only sold the last sweater you knitted but the lady was so pleased that she ordered a muffler and gloves to match."

I smiled. "Looks like God has already started to answer my prayers."

"You are right! And this may be a solution. With your knitting ability, Chung Syn, perhaps you can earn enough to pay part of your own tuition. Are you willing to work for your room and board?"

"I'll do anything . . . *anything* to stay!"

"Then I will discuss the matter with our new principal when she arrives next fall. Until then the cook can use another pair of hands in the kitchen." At the door Miss Wong stopped and called over her shoulder. "Guess I'd better write to your father and tell him that you won't be coming home."

That summer's agenda was work—helping with cooking and housecleaning chores during the day, filling orders for stockings, gloves, mufflers, and sweaters at night. Sometimes my needles clicked until the early morning hours. When I did get to bed the humidity and oppressive heat made sleep nearly impossible. Weakened by lack of sleep and overwork, I came down with malaria, and its lingering symptoms left me with chills one minute and a burning fever the next. Some mornings it was all I could do to drag myself out of bed, yet I was afraid to tell anyone—lest they send me home.

As usual, persistence paid off. When school was ready to start in the fall my back tuition was all paid up, a few dorm fees had been taken care of for the next semester, and my symptoms of malaria had vanished with the first flurry of snow. The future looked bright—until I was called to the principal's office unexpectedly.

"Chung Syn," she explained, "the school is in financial difficulty. The funds we previously received from America have been drastically cut." Even before she finished I had a premonition of what was coming next. "As you know, we have five orphans who are totally dependent on us for support. These youngsters have no place else to live, so naturally we must care for them first." She paused. "It takes money to operate a school. For months we have been cutting our overhead costs, hoping it wouldn't be necessary to turn worthy students away because of financial problems." Her voice softened. "It breaks my heart to tell you, but the scholarship fund is completely drained."

"Can't I stay . . . until the end of the year? I was hoping to graduate."

Miss Robbins leaned forward and took my hand in hers. "Believe me, Chung Syn, this was not an easy decision to make. No one wants to see you finish the course more than I. You are a most conscientious student . . . a courageous young lady. We are hoping for further contributions." Miss Robbins squeezed my hand. "If and when they come," she added, "you will be the first one called back."

I thanked her and slowly walked to the dorm. Earlier that morning graduation had seemed a certainty. Now everything had exploded. Obviously Miss Robbins didn't understand the situation at home. If the financial stress was bad here, it was even worse for my family. How could I return and be an added burden for father? There had to be another way out!

Since first coming to Pyongyang I had cherished a dream of someday helping the blind of Korea achieve recognition. I had a burning desire to prove to scoffers that physically handicapped people are not necessarily retarded, but sometimes have keener minds and greater insights than those who have no disabilities. How could I make those dreams come true without first completing my own education? No one would listen to a blind beggar!

Tears of disappointment and desperation dampened my pillow that night. For hours I wrestled with this latest setback, wracking my brain for a workable solution. Perhaps I could find a full-time job and drop out of school for a year, then enroll again when I had saved enough money. But who would hire a blind girl without skills or experience? Where would I live in the meantime?

Insidious doubts began to creep into my mind, and for the first time I questioned the goodness of God. Was my faith misplaced? Had I been betrayed by my heavenly Father? It didn't seem fair or possible that a God of love would dangle the promise of a better life before me, then snatch it away without reason.

I remembered the trials of Job but with the myopia of youth, ignored the fact that he had remained faithful, refusing to wallow in self-pity. In the past my own faith had been strong too, each crisis bringing me closer to the Lord. But lately my prayers seemed to bounce off the ceiling. *No one* cared about my problems, I reasoned, not even God!

While I lay there worrying about the future and wondering what to do next, thoughts of suicide sneaked into my mind as stealthily as a thief in the night. A small voice inside taunted, *Why go on? There is no way an uneducated girl, blind and alone, can make it on her own! You may as well end the struggle now—once and for all.*

At first pangs of guilt kept the thoughts vague and at bay. I had been taught that the spark of life given by our Creator is sacred, and no one has the right to take it away—no one but the Giver himself. Yet fear and frustration replaced reason.

Immediately I began to make plans. How could I do "it" without arousing suspicion? There were several possibilities. Poison would be fast, although obtaining it might be difficult. What about hanging? Judas Iscariot had selected this way out, but did I want to put myself in the same category as that despicable traitor? Quickly discarding that method, I decided that drowning would suit me best.

Once each week our janitor filled the school bathtub with water, then built a fire underneath to heat it. This oriental-style tub was designed for communal bathing—large enough for several to use at the same time and deep enough to end my misery.

Everyone in the dorm looked forward to bath day, for it was a time to socialize as well as to bathe. When the anticipated day finally arrived, I packed my belongings, tied them in neat bundles, and went outside to collect some heavy stones to weight the pockets and hem of my skirt. At dinner that evening I told the girls I would be leaving for home soon. They all seemed sad, especially my roommates, who were as close as sisters. Later I joined them to take what was to be our last bath together.

"I wish you weren't going home," Myung-Eh lamented as we scrubbed each other's back. "I'll miss you, Chung Syn."

Suddenly the finality of what I was about to do and the eventual consequences of self-destruction hit me, full force. All I could manage to mumble was, "I'll miss you, too, Myung-Eh."

Later that evening, when my roommates had settled down for the night, I pretended to sleep while waiting for the dorm supervisor to make her rounds. At precisely 10:30 her footsteps sounded outside our door, paused momentarily, then faded into the distance.

Now it was safe for me to carry out my plans!

Several minutes later, as I stood beside the tub asking God to forgive me for what I was about to do, a brilliant beam of light seemed to penetrate the darkness. Startled by the strange sensation, I rubbed my eyes and strained to see.

"Stop, Chung Syn," an inner voice admonished. "Don't do this dreadful thing. You'll regret it!"

Guilt swept over me like a tidal wave. But before I could recover from the shock, the uncanny illusion of light disappeared—as quickly as it had come. Now more frightened and confused than ever, I sucked in my breath and stepped into the water. As it closed around me, the same gentle voice asked, "Don't you trust me, Chung Syn? Haven't I always met you needs? Then why doubt me now?"

Was the Lord Himself rebuking me for taking matters into my own hands? Or was this only the voice of my conscience? Regardless, I realized I wanted no part of suicide! Suddenly life seemed very precious—and worth fighting for. Struggling to free myself from the weighted skirt, I gasped for air, swallowing a mouthful of soapy water before popping to the surface.

Moments later, still shivering from the cold and feeling as waterlogged as a soggy sponge, I crawled under the covers of my own bed and opened a Braille copy of the Gospel of John to the first verse of chapter fourteen. With trembling fingers I read its familiar words: "Do not let your hearts be troubled. Trust in God; trust also in me."

How could I have been such a doubting Thomas?

"Forgive me, dear Lord, for doubting," I whispered into the darkness. "If you really want me to go home, I am willing. . . . But you know, Lord, how much I would like to stay. If you will help me get a good education, I promise never to marry and to serve you faithfully for the rest of my life."

With a warm glow and memories of my soul-searching experience uppermost in my mind, I fell asleep. During the night I dreamed that a nobleman gave me a beautiful bouquet of flowers. As I admired them, the petals wilted, one by one, and fluttered to the ground. Noting my disappointment the nobleman smiled and said, "Never mind, Chung Syn. Earthly flowers will perish, but eternity's gifts are everlasting. Someday, when you live in one of those mansions Jesus has gone to prepare, your vision will be restored . . . and you will see Him, face to face."

Who could ask for more?

CHAPTER 8

A Promise
To Keep

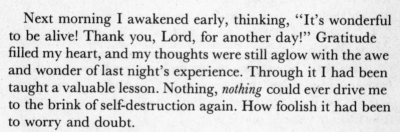

Next morning I awakened early, thinking, "It's wonderful to be alive! Thank you, Lord, for another day!" Gratitude filled my heart, and my thoughts were still aglow with the awe and wonder of last night's experience. Through it I had been taught a valuable lesson. Nothing, *nothing* could ever drive me to the brink of self-destruction again. How foolish it had been to worry and doubt.

All the fears and frustrations that had caused me to attempt suicide were gone. I felt relaxed! Relieved! Excited about the future and all that it held. Surely God had spared me for some special reason that He alone knew.

The six o'clock bell shattered my reverie. In a few seconds sounds of girlish voices and activity rushed through the open door. As usual my roommates needed prodding.

"Good morning, sleepy heads," I greeted, giving Myung-Eh's covers an insistent tug. "Time to get up."

"Go away," she mumbled, pulling the quilt over her head.

"Sorry, Cinderella, but if you sleep much longer your coach will turn into a pumpkin. I can smell the millet cooking."

Yun-Soon turned over and stifled a yawn. "How come you're so bright and cheerful, Chung Syn?"

Myung-Eh was wide awake now. "I never know what to expect from you next," she announced, her feet hitting the floor with a thud. "Yesterday you were crying about leaving. Today you're happy as a nightingale. What's come over you, Chung Syn? I don't understand you at all."

Why try and explain? Neither girl knew what had happened the night before. Somehow I couldn't bring myself to tell them of my suicide attempt, nor of my soul-searching encounter with the Lord. Maybe someday. Not now. It was still too personal. Besides, they would probably laugh at the vow I made to serve God and never marry—if He would help me get a good education. My roommates had plenty of money and no worries. Only the faculty knew what a strain it had been for me to try and scrape together enough cash to stay in school.

I dressed and made my bed with enthusiasm, feeling strangely buoyant and expectant. A weight had slipped from my shoulders. For some unexplainable reason I sensed that my school days were not yet over. Maybe it was a premonition, or just wishful thinking. But I had an uncanny feeling that good news was on its way.

In the dining hall, classmates inquired about my plans. One asked, "When are you leaving?"

With a smile of confidence I turned to her. "The train leaves at two this afternoon." I was tempted to add, "but I won't be on it."

As the morning passed my expectancy grew. I felt as though I had a divinely arranged appointment, but the when, where, of who of it eluded me. While waiting I checked to see that my belongings were all packed and restlessly wandered from one room to another, saying good-by to our maid and caretaker. The dorm clock struck ten . . . eleven . . . twelve. Still nothing had happened.

At 12:30 the office clerk called my name. "Hurry, Chung Syn. The dean wants to see you. She says it's urgent." Was this the summons I had been expecting?

When I rushed into the office, Miss Ahn greeted me cordially. "Come in and sit down, Chung Syn. I have something important to talk over with you."

"Yes?" I exhaled.

"You are trembling. Relax. I have good news. Two new students arrived on campus this morning. They are sisters, both born blind, and this is their first trip away from the family. Already the little girls are terribly homesick." Miss Ahn went on to tell me that the children had come all the way from Manchuria to attend our school. "They are very young and will need someone to look after them for a while. Fortunately the youngsters' father is able to pay for the special care they will require. I talked it over with the staff, and we were just wondering. . . ." Miss Ahn paused thoughtfully, and the uncertainty caused my heart literally to bounce. Impulsively I scooted to the edge of my chair while waiting for her to continue.

"Yes?" I asked hopefully.

"We were wondering if you could be their big sister and look after the girls . . . without neglecting your own studies. If you think it would be too much for you, we'll understand."

"I have had experience taking care of children, Miss Ahn. Of course I can do it."

"They will need help with their homework and someone to take them to classes . . . until they learn their way around."

"That will be no problem at all," I assured her. "And thank you very much. You know that I will do anything, anything at all to stay in school."

The dean hugged me. "I have confidence in you, and everyone on the staff was happy when this unexpected opportunity arose."

A short while later I was introduced to In-Young and
Oh-Young. They were easy to love—sweet, shy, and eager for
attention. They called me "big sister" and clung to my hands,
one on each side, as I took them to inspect and become
familiar with our new living quarters. We had been assigned
to a large sunny room which we were to share with one older
student.

Even before the girls were comfortably settled and their
trunks unpacked, I realized that the task ahead was not going
to be as simple as it sounded. Although they were sweet and
cooperative, neither of the children had been thoroughly toilet
trained. Invariably they would wait too long, or get nervous
and lose control, first one and then the other making a mess
for me to clean up. I spent so much time in the laundry room
that my own studies did begin to suffer, and my patience grew
short.

About ten days after their arrival our dorm maid called me
into the washroom. Her voice raised in anger: "Chung Syn,
these clothes aren't clean. If you don't start doing a better job
I will tell the supervisor." Without another word she flung the
soiled clothes on the floor and flaunted out.

I was humiliated and discouraged—but determined not to
give up. How could I scrub out stains without first being able
to see them? There had to be a solution! As I gathered up the
girls' soggy clothes and whispered a prayer, past incidents
came to mind, past challenges that had been conquered. How
had I learned to braid my own hair, to sew, to thread needles?
By patience and practice, of course! Was I going to be
defeated now—by a heap of dirty clothes? Never!

While the children ate dinner I filled two basins with water,
submerged clean clothes in one and soiled garments in the
other. Then I began comparing the two. At first they felt the
same, but gradually my sensitive fingers detected a slight
difference. So I soaped what seemed to be the offensive spots

and started to scrub, then carefully rinsed and hung the clothes back on the line.

Next morning the maid examined my work again. "I'm amazed," she exclaimed. "You haven't missed a spot. How did you do it?"

I smiled and said, "Thank you," but decided not to tell her that perseverance and prayer had provided the solution.

In-Young and Oh-Young's father paid for my room and board, as well as tuition. Although I had no cash for incidentals, my classmates were always generous. When someone discovered that I was out of paper she would slip me several sheets and tell the others. Soon I would have enough to make into a notebook. The girls also shared their clothes, and the dorm supervisor paid me several *chun* (cents) a month for doing extra housekeeping chores. This gave me a little cash for Sunday school offerings and emergencies.

I budgeted my time, but there were never enough hours in which to complete my responsibilities and still get adequate rest. Afternoons I tutored the girls, and nights, when they were in bed, I did the laundry. Fortunately I had become a fast reader and could skim over the raised dots with lightning speed, but many times I fell asleep while studying.

Because my resistance was low I became the target for one infection and sore throat after another. Doctors decided a tonsillectomy might help. It was performed without benefit of an anesthetic! Next I developed chronic pleurisy, aggravated by a deep, congested cough. When my lungs filled with fluid doctors drained the pleural cavity. What a dreaded ordeal!

That winter Pyongyang's population shivered from the most severe temperatures on record, and my flimsy, cotton-lined jacket provided little protection. When my physical condition didn't improve our dorm supervisor suggested I go to the hospital.

"In-Young and Oh-Young need me," I insisted. "They are

afraid to be left alone. In a day or two I'll feel fine again."
Although the girls were now toilet trained, they still felt
insecure around others.

The supervisor finally agreed. "All right, Chung Syn. But
you must promise to stay in bed for a few days." Bed rest,
however, wasn't enough. In time I did go to Kitok (Christ
Hospital) and stayed for more than three weeks, recovering
from acute pneumonia. For several days my condition was
quite serious, but classmates prayed. And the Great Physician
took over.

During convalescence I memorized Isaiah 40:31. It gave me
encouragement then and is still one of my favorite verses:
"They who wait on the LORD will renew their strength. They
shall soar on wings like eagles; they will run and not grow
weary, they will walk and not be faint." How many times
through the years I have leaned on that promise!

Teachers and classmates from Chung-Jin came by the
hospital daily, bringing fruit, cards, books, and assignments.
With their help I was able to keep up with my classwork, and
by the semester's end had completed the six-year course.

I was now a candidate for graduation from grade school.

CHAPTER 9

New Challenges

Near the semester's end, I returned to the dorm one afternoon and was greeted by an unexpected visitor.

"Hello, Chung Syn."

"Father!" I exclaimed. "Is it *really* you?"

"Yes, *ahga*," he laughed, crossing the room to clasp me in his arms. It had been years since anyone had called me *ahga*! I clung to him, almost afraid he would vanish if I let go. His endearing presence and the coarse homespun of his jacket against my face brought back an avalanche of memories.

"Can you stay for graduation?"

"Yes," father answered. "We will all be here."

"*We*? I don't understand. Father, is something wrong?"

He cleared his throat. "Your mother and I have moved to Pyongyang."

"Why? Will you be happy living in the city?"

"We lost our land," he said, "and I thought conditions might be better here. We've rented a room on the other side of town for two *won* a month."

"Are you working?"

Father evaded the question. "Steady jobs aren't easy to find, . . . but sometimes I carry baggage at the train station."

When I visited my family the following weekend, I found them living in poverty. Their shabby room in the tenement house had little furniture and bare cupboards. When Yu-nok and Teuk-Choon hugged me, I wept because they were both so skinny. Mother was gone. My brother and sister told me she had been selling vegetables from door-to-door in order to earn money for rice. When she came home empty-handed, the children went hungry.

Daily, from midnight until 1 A.M., I prayed for them, asking God to give father steady employment. Knowing I couldn't attend middle school without financial assistance, I also prayed about my own future. So much depended on my getting a good education!

Miss Choe thought my high grade-point average might qualify me for a scholarship with the Presbyterian Missionary Society, so she made an appointment for the two of us to see Rev. and Mrs. Hill. The interview was disappointing. At that time blind students weren't admitted to middle schools, and the Hills doubted that my health would permit me to complete the strenuous course.

A few days later, however, Mrs. Hill invited me back. "I haven't been able to dismiss your face from my mind," she said. "Your wistful smile has haunted me since the day you were here." She hesitated for a moment. "You seem so eager . . . and sincere. But how could you possibly keep up with the sighted students?"

"Nothing is impossible . . with God's help."

"You are a very determined young lady," Mrs. Hill conceded, "and how can I argue with such logic?"

I left that interview with my head in the clouds and the missionary's words still ringing in my ears: "If you can qualify for middle school, Chung Syn, my husband and I will take care of your tuition for the first year."

Grade school graduation day finally arrived. I was so excited that I completely forgot my embarrassment over wearing borrowed shoes and an old skirt mother had dyed black to match the other girls'. Each blind student was led to the platform by a sighted graduate, who also nudged us when it was time to stand or to bow. How proud I felt to receive a certificate of honor along with my diploma. Father was proud, too. Even mother seemed pleased!

When entrance exams started at Soong-Yee Middle School I joined seven hundred other hopefuls to compete for one of the ninety openings. After an anxious week of waiting, results were posted on the bulletin board. When my name didn't appear on the list, Miss Choe insisted on taking me to see the school principal. "You at least deserve an explanation," she fumed.

Miss Swallun assured us that it wasn't a question of my ability. "As a matter of fact, you did remarkably well on the exams. But our teachers aren't willing to accept blind students."

Righteous indignation gave me courage to challenge the decision. "I may be blind, Miss Swallun, but my test scores prove that I can do the work. Won't you please reconsider?"

"You don't seem to understand," she persisted. "Our teachers aren't trained to teach handicapped students."

I decided to try another approach. "Do you believe the Bible?"

"Of course I do," she stammered.

"Then you know that Jesus helped handicapped people on many occasions. Did He ever pass by the lame or the blind without showing compassion?" I stopped abruptly, shocked by my own boldness.

"Why do you ask?"

"I need your help, Miss Swallun. If the teachers won't give me a seat, may I stand outside and listen to their lectures? Could they leave the doors ajar? Please? Is that asking too much?"

Her next words gave me hope. "Thank you, Chung Syn, for teaching me a lesson. Tomorrow we're having another faculty meeting. Perhaps staff members can be persuaded to change their minds."

Somehow Miss Swallun convinced them! The school administrators gave me a year's probation, and I resolved to prove their confidence had not been misplaced—even if it meant studying day and night.

I made arrangements to continue living at Chung-Jin in order to care for my two young charges. The little sisters had matured considerably during the past two years. They now needed less supervision and could walk the short distance to school by themselves. Afternoons and early evenings I planned to tutor them and then do my own studying when they were tucked in for the night. That left Saturdays for catching up with the laundry and cleaning.

Everything was falling into place. Several sighted friends agreed to guide me—until I could learn identifying landmarks along the unfamiliar route. After only three days, I decided to try traveling alone but made a wrong turn and became hopelessly lost. Too sensitive to ask for help I stumbled along until a seminary student noticed my confusion and insisted on escorting me himself.

I quickly learned to count corners more carefully and to make mental notes that would help identify surroundings later on. After a little practice I was able to make the trip through traffic or winter weather without losing my sense of direction.

All the girls at Soong-Yee were required to wear uniforms, but where would I get money to buy one? The answer wasn't long in coming. Sinjune, a young woman of my acquaintance who had recently graduated, gave me a slightly-worn, slightly-large jacket. A few alterations made it fit fine. Two weeks later the principal herself presented me with a blouse, black skirt, and a pair of white rubber shoes. Words failed me! It was impossible to express my gratitude. Everyone had been so kind!

Braille books had to be special-ordered, and it took three weeks for mine to arrive. In the meantime I scrupulously made notes and tried to memorize as much material as possible during class. My favorite teacher seemed to sense each time I became discouraged. This perceptive woman patiently answered questions and volunteered to tutor me after school when problems were particularly difficult. Others were inclined to watch and wait with skepticism to see how long it would take me to give up.

Miss Swallun, aware of my tenacious nature and ever-present fear of rejection, was generous with praise. Each compliment or word of encouragement spurred me on, and by the semester's end my grade-point average was an unwavering 95 percent.

Oh-Young and In-Young were scheduled to spend the summer months in Manchuria with their parents, and I planned to stay in our room, helping with housekeeping chores as usual. Just before the girls left, however, I received a letter from their mother. She thanked me for taking good care of her daughters and told me she felt they were now old enough to manage by themselves.

The news came as a shock! Once again I was without work, and since the room we had shared was needed for incoming students, I also had to find housing. But how? Where? Father suggested that I move in with them, at least temporarily. Since no other solution was in sight I agreed, but with great reluctance. My presence in the overcrowded flat would not be welcomed.

Eager to be self-supporting, I applied for work at the Soon Sill College workshop. During my interview the supervisor, Mrs. Park asked if I'd had any experience carding wool.

"No, ma'am. But I'm willing to learn." She immediately put me to work making yarn balls. After a few hours my fingers began to swell. And my nose itched! Nothing about the monotonous job was challenging—but my weekly paycheck made the situation tolerable.

Several evenings later I returned home and found the children crying from hunger. Mother and father were both gone, so I took Yu-nok with me to ask Mrs. Park for a salary advance. She loaned me fifty *chun,* and I purchased ten pounds of rice, three cucumbers, and some sweets for the children. That night they both went to bed with full stomachs, and our parents returned to a pot of steaming rice. Never again did mother call me a "blind and useless daughter."

City summers were hot and humid, and this one was no exception. Working with wool accentuated the heat, but with a family of five to feed there was no way I could take a few days off before school started. Instead I prayed and put the future in God's hands.

"My father will give you whatever you ask in my name," Jesus promised. "Ask, and you will receive, and your joy will be complete" (John 16:23, 24).

I had asked before and God had provided according to His own perfect timetable—never too soon or too late. Why worry now?

CHAPTER 10

Middle School

Although father hadn't found steady employment when school started, I decided to trust God and move on campus anyway. There was nothing I could do to solve my parents' problems, and, if I stayed, it would be impossible for me to concentrate on studies with all the noise, confusion, and uncertainties.

By working afternoons at the farm and with careful management, I could make enough to cover dorm costs. Mrs. Hill had assured me the missionary scholarship would still be available. Other things—feminine frills and little luxuries—I could do without. My clothes were clean and mended; what difference did a perfect fit or matching colors make?

I had a far greater concern—the overwhelming, ever-present fear of rejection. Would seeing students accept me as a roommate? Could I overcome my own timidity and make new friends?

Mother's well-meaning remarks did nothing to reinforce my confidence. "You'd better stay with us, Chung Syn," she advised. "Do you want those rich girls to laugh at your

patched clothes and feel sorry for you?" The last thing I
wanted was pity!

In early September I moved to the school campus to get
oriented before the start of classes. It was like stepping into a
whole new world. I felt lost and alone. My two roommates
were uncomfortable around me, since neither had known a
blind person before; and when I stepped into the room, their
conversations stopped. Knowing they were looking me over,
made me feel ill at ease.

At Chung-Jin, blindness had been a bond. Here it set me
apart. I missed the camaraderie of caring friends. As I tapped
my way along the corridors, a few students politely
murmured, "Hello," but no one offered assistance.

Mrs. Hill had tried to warn me: "Don't be disappointed if
it's hard to get acquainted at first. It will just take time . . .
and patience."

She was right. It did take time . . . and lots of patience. But
I was determined to prove to my peers and teachers that
physically handicapped people have the same fears and
frustrations, the same desires and dreams, as everyone else.

At Chung-Jin I had learned the art of making alterations. A
tuck here, a pleat there, or a few gathers around the waist
could make hand-me-downs fit—more or less. But some
things couldn't be improvised.

"Why haven't you made up your bed?" the dorm maid
asked. I blushed with embarrassment. "Don't you have
sheets?" she asked, lowering her voice so the others couldn't
hear. I shook my head, and she said no more. But the
following evening I returned from work to find a stack of
neatly folded linens on the foot of my bed.

"It's nothing," the dorm maid insisted when I tried to
thank her. "I found some extra bedding in the linen closet and
thought you might as well use it." When I turned to leave she
added, "If you need anything else, please let me know."

I didn't tell her those sheets were an answer to prayer!

Before long I was settled into a busy school schedule—attending classes in the morning, working at the farm afternoons, and returning to the dorm after everyone else had eaten supper. Evenings I crammed. There was seldom time to socialize, but I did not have time to worry about a lack of close friends. Every minute was spent poring over my Braille textbooks and stylus. When classmates went on outings or field trips, as they often did during nice weather, I stayed behind to study. Going to church on Sunday was my only diversion.

Shortly after *Iptong* (the beginning of winter) Pyongyang's temperature dipped below zero. Icy winds whipped the city streets, and foot travelers crouched to keep from being toppled by the Siberian-like blasts. Sometime earlier the other students had switched to winter uniforms—blue serge skirts, heavy jackets, and woolen coats. But I was still wearing summer cottons. Each day my walk to the outskirts of town seemed longer, the temperature more frigid. Although I needed a new uniform in the worst way my budget couldn't be stretched to purchase one.

When Miss Swallun heard about my dilemma she called me to her office. The outer door was open when I arrived.

"Sit down, Chung Syn, while I finish sorting these papers," she said, "It will only take a minute."

I leaned back in the comfortable chair, smiling to myself and remembering the first time I had come here with Miss Choe. The audacity with which I had challenged this gracious woman that day made my cheeks turn crimson, even now. Then she had been a total stranger. Today Miss Swallun was my friend, and without her assistance I would not be a student at Soong-Yee!

Miss Swallun's warm, friendly voice brought me back to the present. "I understand you need a winter uniform," she said, pinpointing my problem in a straightforward way. "Is that true?" I nodded. "Why didn't you tell me?"

"I didn't want to bother you, Miss Swallun. I am already indebted to you."

"Nonsense!" she exclaimed. "You owe me nothing. Tomorrow I shall see about ordering material for your uniform."

"I don't have money to pay you right now, but maybe each week I could . . ."

"Forget it, Chung Syn. Let's just say this is a very small gift of gratitude . . . from me to you."

I tried to protest. "But you have done too much already. How can I ever repay you?"

"By taking care of yourself." Her voice was gentle. "Your courage is a challenge to me and everyone else. You have contributed something very special to our student body."

"Thank you. I'll study hard and try not to disappoint you."

"You've already made me proud, but I am concerned about your health. You look tired and tense. Please try and get to bed a bit earlier. I'm sure your roommates will cooperate."

No use telling her that they were asleep long before I put my books aside every night, I decided. She might scold!

"By the way, are you taking cod-liver oil?" she asked as an afterthought.

I shuddered.

The principal laughed. "It's not that bad, really. You should take a spoonful every day."

Within a short time the dorm supervisor delivered a package to my room. It contained blue serge material for my uniform—and a huge bottle of something that smelled horrible.

"These things are from the principal," she said. "Miss Swallun told me to give them to you . . . in exchange for a very special gift you once gave her. I don't understand what she meant. Do you?"

I smiled and nodded.

The following March I completed my probation period at Soong-Yee. It had been a rough year, and I felt utterly drained. Yet nothing could negate or lessen the thrill of hearing my name called during assembly as one who was receiving an academic award and status as a regular student.

This was more than a personal triumph. It had actually set a precedent and, in essence, was a victory for other blind hopefuls who had been turned away from secondary schools. If one sightless student had climbed the academic ladder successfully, why not others? Perhaps someone, someday, might make it to the top rung!

Equally gratifying was the casual and warm way sighted students were now treating me. I was included in after-class discussions and was sometimes asked for advice. Girls from the dorm invited me on outings, although I was generally too busy to accept, and they insisted on sharing fruit and other goodies from home.

One morning a friend from across the hall fell into step beside my roommate and me. Moon, a personable and out-going girl, was excitedly opening a package she had just picked up at the post office.

"Look, Chung Syn," she exclaimed, handing me a soft, silky scarf as we walked. "Mother sent me this. Isn't it simply elegant?"

"Oh yes, Moon. It's very lovely," I agreed, fingering the soft folds of fabric. "Tell me, what are the colors?"

"I'm sorry!" Moon apologized, linking her arm through mine. "Believe it or not, I sometimes *forget* that you can't see!" Impulsively she squeezed my arm. Remembering Mrs. Hill's earlier prediction, I smiled and said nothing.

It was so good to be accepted!

That same day the school counselor stopped me on campus. "Chung Syn, I would like to talk with you for a moment," she said. "Do you have a free period?" I nodded and followed Miss Loo to her office, wondering all the way what she had in mind.

"Is something wrong?" I finally asked, unable to contain my curiosity a minute longer.

"Wrong?" she laughed. "Indeed not! I am very proud of you."

"Thanks, *sun seng nim,* but my instructors deserve the credit. You have all been so helpful."

"That's why I called you here. Several of your teachers believe it would be a waste of time for you to attend second-year classes."

My heart sank! "Do you mean . . . I can't stay at Soong-Yee?"

"Quite the contrary," Miss Loo laughed. "We think you should *skip* a grade . . . and start third-year classes in the fall."

Her words should have filled me with pride and pleasure. But they didn't! Instead I was seized with panic! What if I flunked out? Math had been my most difficult subject so far, since unseen geometric symbols were hard to visualize. Could I cope with trigonometry? All sorts of negatives flashed through my mind.

I blurted out my fears. "Miss Loo, may I please stay with my own class?"

"Why, Chung Syn? If you're worried about making new friends. . . ."

"Oh no, it isn't that!"

"Then what is troubling you, dear?"

"I'm afraid. What if . . . what if I don't do well? I'm attending school on a scholarship, you know. What if I let my sponsors down?"

"Don't worry. Your teachers think you can handle

advanced classes. If you find it's too difficult, let me know."

I still wasn't convinced and went to talk it over with Mrs. Hill.

"I agree with your counselor," she assured me.

Mr. Hill, a man of few words, said, "Chung Syn, don't worry so much about what others think. Your first responsibility is to God. As long as you stay in His will the Lord will bless and guide you. Mrs. Hill and I learned that lesson years ago. Some thought we were crazy for wanting to be missionaries in Korea. But we both knew, deep in our hearts, that this was where God wanted us, and we've never regretted coming. My advice to you, young lady, is to follow God's leading."

"And my advice to you, Harry Hill, is to be on your way," his wife laughingly admonished, "unless you want to be late for your appointment."

Later my hostess and I finished the conversation over cups of steaming tea and a plate of sugar cookies. "I believe that God has work for you to do, Chung Syn . . . right here in Korea. For us time is running out, but your life is still ahead of you. Funny thing, when I was your age time seemed to stand still. Now I realize that days disappear as quickly as the morning mist, and suddenly we're old." There was a sweet wistfulness in my friend's voice as she spoke.

"You will always seem young to me, Mrs. Hill—young and lovely."

"That's because you can't see the wrinkles," she laughed, "or the gray in my hair. Believe me, my mirror isn't so kind."

"Maybe that's one of the compensations for being blind," I mused aloud. "It's better to see friends through the eyes of love. I've learned to judge people by *what they are*, not by how they look. Yes, where friends are concerned, it is a blessing to be blind!"

Mrs. Hill was thoughtful for a moment. "You know there is

a passage in the Bible that says just that. God warned Samuel not to judge a man by his countenance. "Man looks at the outward appearance," he said, "but the LORD looks at the heart" (1 Sam. 16:7).

My American friend moved closer and slipped her arm around my shoulders. "Chung Syn, you are a lovely young lady, a young lady with inner beauty and depth of character that doesn't meet the eye. I am so glad that God brought you into my life!"

Is it any wonder that I learned to love this wonderful missionary friend very, very much? To me both Mary and Harry Hill epitomized "America the beautiful—land of the free and the home of the brave."

CHAPTER 11

Growing Pains

During the monsoon season, treacherous winds sweep across eastern Asia, assailing ships at sea and battering coastlines with reckless vengeance. Because of these torrential downpours, Korea receives thirty-five to forty inches of rainfall. Sometimes several inches pelt the land within a few hours.

Rice farmers welcome the rains, since paddies must be flooded before tender seedlings are set out; but city dwellers dread the sticky weather and sloshy conditions. As rain pelts the steaming streets and sidewalks, the temperature and humidity rise. Foot traffic is virtually halted.

In the late 1930s, many of Pyongyang's most affluent families—Japanese plutocrats and members of the governing echelon—lived in country homes or lakeview resorts during this season to escape sweltering city temperatures. Since many students were from out of town, they also returned home at the conclusion of spring semester to avoid the uncomfortable summers. A few, like myself, remained at the dorm all year.

Late one August evening I returned to campus after a busy day at the workshop and was hailed by the dorm maid. "You received a letter from Miss Swallun today," she told me. "Shall I read it to you?"

"Please do." Miss Swallun was spending her vacation at the seashore, and I missed her.

"Dear Chung Syn," she read, "I hope you are relaxing this summer and not working too hard. I am writing to tell you some good news. The General Students' Association has decided to pay half of your living expenses starting next semester. I will also continue to provide your uniforms and cod-liver oil."

The maid stopped abruptly. "Cod-liver oil?" she asked.

I nodded and broke into a grin. "Miss Swallun insists that I take the nasty stuff. She says it will keep me healthy."

The next semester was a time of growth, both spiritually and academically. Without the constant pressure of unpaid bills, I had more time to study and become a part of campus life. Other students soon accepted me warmly and without restraint. My roommates and I became close friends, and with Miss Swallun coaching me after class, the dreaded trigonometry wasn't so difficult after all.

Since I had first mastered Braille and *Hangul,* reading had been a great joy. Nights when my nerves were too taut to sleep, I read in bed— such classics as *Quo Vadis,* and the works of St. Francis of Assisi. Although schools weren't permitted to teach Korean history, and we only studied Japanese literature, one of the "forbidden books" somehow found its way into a Braille edition. I checked out the autobiography of Ae-In Bong (a Korean nobleman), reading and relishing it from cover to cover. While flipping the final pages a surge of national pride stirred within me.

Someday would my people and country be free again?

Music was then and still is a very meaningful part of my life.

As a child I had sung hymns in our little village church and had loved listening to the music of the traditional folk dances at festivals. I kept time with my hands as musicians played the *komungo* (zither) and *piri* (double reed oboes). Those were meaningful moments, now safely stored in memory.

During my third year at Soong-Yee I was able to study voice with Miss Loots, and that one hour was the high point of each week.

"You have a lovely voice," she told me, "with intense versatility and timbre. I'm certain your personality and style of delivery would be endearing to audiences. Have you considered music as a profession?"

I assured her that such a thing had never crossed my mind.

"Then you might give the idea some thought. After graduation from high school perhaps you could attend a good music conservatory." Miss Loots' words were, indeed, music to my ears, and from that day forward I practiced with diligence!

Mother and father, unable to cope with pressures of city life, returned to the country. Now there was no one except Mrs. Hill with whom I could talk over personal problems. Not wanting to bother this busy woman, I sometimes poured my frustrations out on paper. Most Korean students kept a diary, and the entries in mine during those tumultuous days reflected all the uncertainties of a typical teenager standing at the threshold of young womanhood—with many unanswered questions.

No one had prepared me for puberty; I didn't understand the physical and psychological changes taking place within. My emotions during those years were unpredictable and sometimes as breathtaking as a roller coaster ride. I was still small for my age, and, although making decisions and assuming responsibilities beyond my years had given me a measure of maturity, beneath the surface, I sometimes felt like a child.

Adolescence was also a time of soul-searching. *Was there really a God of love? Did all things work together for good? How could I be sure?* I decided to study the Scriptures in depth to either prove or disprove the Bible's validity. "Study to show thyself approved unto God," Timothy had said, "a workman that needeth not to be ashamed, rightly dividing the word of truth" (2 Tim. 2:15 KJV).

As I studied, my faith grew. Things once questioned or half-heartedly believed were now a positive reality. I set goals for myself and tried to memorize as many passages as possible, not realizing that those very verses would later sustain me through one of the most trying and traumatic years of my life.

On warm evenings I enjoyed strolling through the carefully groomed gardens on campus. During spring and early summer months the air was always filled with the sweet scent of flowers. I learned to identify each blossom by its fragrance. Sometimes I just sat by the fountain, dipped my fingers in its cool waters, and reflected on the past.

Memories of my sighted days were always the sweetest. Had it really been a dozen years since Choon and I romped through the countryside in search of butterflies and adventure? Remembering the beautiful pink coat Sunbi made always brought a smile. How was she now? Were she and her husband happily married? Were they struggling to make a living? It made me sad to recall that our parents had once been poor but happy. Why had their dreams turned into a nightmare? Circumstances had contributed—the occupation, poverty, Choon's death, my loss of sight—but mother and father still could be content in spite of everything if only they would *let go and let God* solve their problems.

Moranbong Hill was a favorite place for hikes and picnics. After one class outing, I stayed behind to study outside. The hill was unusually quiet, and a sudden sound, although barely perceptible, distracted me. Was it only a bird's chirp? I raised my head to listen, and hearing it again, went to investigate. Hiding in the bushes was a young, frightened pheasant.

The fledgling made no attempt to escape when I picked it up but seemed content to nestle and hide in the folds of my skirt. On closer examination my fingers found that the little fellow was injured. Some of his head feathers were missing, others were encrusted with blood. Rather than abandon the young pheasant to an eagle or hawk, I carried it back to my room for a drink of water and a bit of rice.

Before my roommates returned I set the revived bird on a ledge near an open window. "All right, my fine feathered friend, it's time to fly back to the woods." The contented bird merely chirped and stayed on his perch. No amount of urging made him move.

How nice it would be to have a pet, I thought to myself, *something of my very own to care for and cuddle.* It was just wishful thinking, of course, but maybe. . . . Suddenly I had an inspiration. "Come along, little bird," I laughed. "It's against the rules to keep you in the dorm. So we're going to see the principal!"

Miss Swallun was sympathetic—as I knew she would be—and offered to care for the injured pheasant. Students and staff alike were puzzled as they walked past her office. For several weeks contented little chirps drifted through an open transom—and no one knew why.

For the next three years I had a variety of roommates, some a pleasure, others a disappointment. One semester a twenty-six-year-old graduate nurse was assigned to my room. Myongsuk had returned to Soong-Yee to take some additional classes. She seemed congenial and understanding, but I sensed that her sympathy for me was superficial.

One day when I stumbled over something she had left in the middle of our room, Myongsuk accused me of being clumsy. "It makes me uncomfortable to live with you, Chung Syn. I'm torn between pity . . . and disgust." All of her animosity spewed forth. "Tell me, have you seen a doctor lately?"

"No, I'm not sick."

"Then I wish you'd stop coughing! You're spreading germs all over the place."

"I'm sorry. I do have a cold, but. . . ."

"It's more than a cold. You sound and look tubercular," Myongsuk retorted. "I'll be glad when the semester is over!" With that barbed comment she stomped out of the room and slammed the door.

Her words stung, but only temporarily. My disgruntled critic soon moved to other quarters, and I quickly forgot her accusations.

CHAPTER 12

A Crucial Decision

The student study group I soon joined met on a regular basis to share notes and ideas. Sometimes we paired up to coach each other for exams. It was a good outlet, giving me an opportunity to socialize as well as study. We all became the best of friends.

One evening during the start of my senior year I dashed to the library straight from work, arriving late and out of breath, my mind on an upcoming exam. The other girls were already there and discussing something in hushed tones. They· sounded quite upset.

"Why all the whispering?" I asked. "What's up?"

"Plenty!" Sinjune answered, her voice rising in a high pitched falsetto. "We're virtually prisoners in our own country. One doesn't know what to expect next!"

"Sh-h-h! Keep your voice down," Soon-Cho cautioned. "Even the walls have ears. Do you want to get us all in trouble?"

"At this point who cares about a little more trouble?" Sinjune retorted. "I'm angry! Absolutely furious!"

"Making a scene won't help," Soon-Cho chided. "We've got to be cautious. The librarian is watching us with an eagle eye."

"Don't worry about Miss Wong. She can be trusted."

"Maybe so, but rules are rules, and we're supposed to be quiet in the library."

"Why not come back to my room?" Ae-douk whispered. "We can sit on the floor if there aren't enough chairs. My roommate's out for the evening . . . so we can be alone. What do you think?"

All of the girls thought it would be a good idea. So Soon-Cho scooped up my Braille books with one hand and grabbed my arm with the other. "Come on Chung Syn. Let's walk together."

After the girls were all comfortably seated oriental-style on the floor, I asked again. "What's all the excitement about? I'm dying to hear. Please . . . tell me why you're so upset?"

"Mr. Kim called an assembly this afternoon while you were at work to announce that Japanese officials have declared a new state religion. From now on we must all worship at Shinto shrines. Do you realize what that means?"

Sinjune's message was slow to sink in. "Shinto? Korea's state religion? But we're Christians. Not even the Emperor can tell us how to worship."

"Don't be too sure," Soon-Cho insisted, tapping her fingers nervously on the table as she spoke. "Buddhist students feel the same way, but all is fair in love and war. At this point we are pawns of the occupation forces."

"I can't believe it!"

"No one could at first, but it's true. They are also asking male students to enlist for duty in the Japanese army."

Korean men serving with enemy troops? A bomb couldn't have had a more devastating effect. At first I was shocked. Then anger took over!

"I'll never bow to Shinto . . . nor worship at pagan shrines. Never! No one can make me!" My impulsive statement was made in haste. We would all have time to consider the consequences during days to come.

After that our school, as well as the city of Pyongyang, was thrown into confusion. Nerves were tense. Tempers flared, but people didn't have the courage to protest. Although church activities were curtailed, doors didn't actually close. Congregations, however, were afraid to be seen worshiping in public. Sooner or later there would come a day of decision. I knew it. Everyone did. But only time would tell the final result.

At the workshop I picked up snatches of conversation and guarded innuendos, enough to sense a growing unrest on the Soon Sill College campus. Then one day smoldering resentments and long suppressed anger popped to the surface like the cork from a bottle of vintage rice wine. Why was everyone so upset? I went to ask Mrs. Park and found her at work in the carding room.

"Students are gathering in front of the administration building. They're angry. What's going on?"

She stopped her work. "I was afraid this would happen. Trouble has been brewing since they removed our principal."

"*Who* did? I don't understand."

"Japanese authorities. They came on campus about two hours ago!"

I rushed back to my own school and learned that our principal had met the same fate. Without considering the consequences, our students decided to join a demonstration on the college campus. Once started, the movement gained momentum with the speed of a runaway rickshaw headed downhill. With the recklessness of youth we protested the removal of our principals, as well as the Shinto decree.

I expected some reprisals. Strangely enough none were imposed. "This is government business. Stick to your studies," school administrators warned. "Protests will cause more trouble. You're only hurting yourselves."

When classes resumed Dean Kim became acting principal. It was difficult for me to concentrate on studies. I kept expecting something more to happen. Nothing did—until two months later—when we were again summoned to the auditorium to hear another mandate.

"By power vested in me by His Royal Majesty, the Emperor of Japan, I hereby declare that it shall be mandatory for every student in Korea to publicly worship at Shinto shrines and to sign a declaration of Shinto faith."

For a few seconds the entire student body was speechless. When the auditorium started to buzz with protests, I slipped quietly out the door and walked to my room in silence, agonizing over this latest development. I loved the Lord with all my heart. How could I denounce Him, after all He had done for me? How could I submit to spiritual subjugation?

After dinner a group of us got together to discuss the decision we all had to make. Some said it was only a formality. "What difference does a silly old paper make?" Moon rationalized. "Nothing will change how we feel inside. Why not sign the declaration? God knows our hearts."

"You're right," Sinjune agreed. "Why make more trouble for ourselves? We may as well sign and forget it. Don't you think so, Chung Syn?"

I shook my head. "I can't compromise about something as important as my faith in God."

That night I lay awake for hours trying to sort things out in my own mind. I knew this was not the first time Korea had been invaded by aggressive and greedy neighbors. The Chinese had come in conquest too, on several occasions. It was they who had introduced the ancient arts, Confucian ethics, and Buddhist religion to our peaceful little country. With the exception of American missionaries who came to

Korea in love, perhaps no other nation had exerted a greater influence on our cultural development than China.

But by comparison, the troops who now occupied our land were crude, coarse, and conniving. They did everything through force and violence. Of all our past enemies, none had been more ruthless. In an effort to colonize and convert us to their ideologies, the Japanese had made one demand after another. Not satisfied to control our land, liberty, and school curriculum, now they wanted to deprive us of our freedom of worship.

While lying there in the dark, snatches of a conversation I'd had with father years before flashed through my mind. "Before you were born," he had said, "I joined the liberation movement. That was in 1919. We were seeking our freedom, not revenge. But those demonstrations were doomed from the start. Against such odds what chance did we have? More than 6,500 Koreans lost their lives. All fine, brave young men. Another sixteen thousand were wounded and some nineteen thousand taken as political prisoners."

"Is that when you went to Russia?" I had asked.

"Yes, I bought a fishing boat and went to sea. Perhaps I was more fortunate than some. Although we lost our home and land, the military police didn't arrest me. But nothing has been the same since." Father had sounded so wistful.

"Would you do the same thing again?"

"Yes. There comes a time in everyone's life when he or she has to make a difficult decision. We must do what we know in our hearts is right, regardless of the cost."

I wanted very much to talk to father now, but that was impossible. Rev. and Mrs. Hill were also gone. They had returned to America for a year's vacation and furlough. Mrs. Hill had written that they wouldn't be back until after my graduation. So this decision, the most important one of my young life, had to be made alone.

My moment-by-moment relationship with Christ was intensely personal, as viable as life itself and as natural as breathing. Through the years, even when separated from my family and surrounded by strangers, I had never been totally alone. In every situation Christ had proven to be close beside me. My first conversation in the morning and last one at night were always with Him. Since early childhood He had been my constant companion, sharing both momentous and trivial moments—victories and defeats, problems and solutions, happiness and heartaches.

I turned to God for all my needs and thanked him for His blessings. He was intricately interwoven into every facet of my life. Denouncing Christ to worship a foreign deity would be as traumatic as cutting off an arm or leg . . . or stopping the beat of my heart.

During devotions the following morning I pled with God for guidance. *Please Lord, please lead me. Give me courage. Keep my faith from wavering.*

God did guide me in an explicit and most convincing manner. As I read the twelfth chapter of Luke my fingers fell on the eighth and ninth verses where Jesus spoke to the multitudes and gave them guidelines to follow: "I tell you, whoever acknowledges me before men, the Son of Man will also acknowledge him before the angels of God. *But he who disowns me before men will be disowned before the angels of God.*"

This was my answer! Peace swept over me. All my doubts disappeared.

Several students dropped out of school before graduation, rather than face the issue. Most, however, did sign the Shinto pledge. I was among the few who did not. A number of our instructors resigned. Others were transferred, and as a consequence, classes were sadly interrupted. Without the leadership of our understanding and supportive principal, we felt like a body without a head.

Not only students suffered at this time. Japanese officials brought pressures to bear on the civilian population as well. Buddhists and Christians alike were subjected to the same indignities. Those of us who refused to bow to Shinto were called *dak dak han mok* (stiff necks).

Harassment was common. Political arrests were made for no apparent reason, and interrogations were brutal. Neighbors often were afraid to trust each other. No one knew for sure who was an informer, who was not.

One week before the date set for graduation, I received an official notice from police headquarters. It said my diploma would be withheld "inasmuch as you have refused to sign the Shinto pledge of faith."

My heart sank, then anger set in. I had struggled and sacrificed for years to graduate from a sighted school. I deserved that piece of paper. A flood of tears followed.

I showed the document to my roommate, and the news spread across campus with the fury of a monsoon wind. Other students wanted to stage a formal demonstration.

"It's not fair," Sinjune fumed. "The least we can do is organize and go to police headquarters. If enough of us protest, maybe they will listen."

"Please don't, Sinjune. It's no use. A demonstration could put everyone in jeopardy. Besides, a diploma isn't that important. They can't take away the things I've learned."

"But it is important," Sinjune insisted. "And something should be done."

Members of the school faculty were irate, but helpless. No one dared defy the police ultimatum—not if they wanted to continue teaching. Privately, however, some did express sympathy and indignation over such an injustice.

One summed up the sentiments of all when she said, "Remember Matthew 5:10, Chung Syn: *'Blessed are those who are persecuted because of righteousness, for theirs is the kingdom of heaven.'* We all admire your courage."

Even the new principal tried to be consoling. She insisted that I attend graduation exercises. "I can't give you a diploma under the circumstances, but," she mused, the hint of a chuckle in her voice, "perhaps we could give you a certificate of completion. Surely no one will object to that." As I turned to leave, Miss Cho added, "If the situation changes in a month or so, I will mail your diploma. See you at graduation."

I thanked her and promised to be present. In a way, I was relieved that the police had denied my diploma instead of taking me into custody. For the past two months I had feared some kind of drastic reprisal. Yes, my punishment could have been much worse!

Knowing that I was the first blind student to complete the course of study at Soong-Yee was compensating in itself—with or without a diploma. And as Miss Cho had said, the certificate would be just as effective if I chose to go on to a university in the future.

Graduation day finally arrived, but there was no one special on hand to share this moment of triumph with me. My family couldn't come because of finances, and the Hills were not returning from America for another week. Being alone at such a time was disappointing, but on March 17, 1938, I marched down the aisle with my classmates and listened to the enthusiastic applause of relatives, as one by one my friends received their diplomas.

CHAPTER 13

The Joys of Serving God

After the commencement services, graduates and their guests gathered in the school auditorium to take pictures, tearfully hugging each other, exchanging addresses, and promising to keep in touch. Saying farewell to classmates seemed so final—like finishing the closing chapter of a good book.

It wasn't easy to be gracious and enthusiastic when others flaunted their diplomas before their admiring relatives and friends. For me, the day had been disappointing from start to finish. After a few minutes I slipped quietly out of the auditorium and strolled toward the deserted dorm.

What next? I wondered while walking along the familiar paths. *Where do I go from here?* Mrs. Park had promised me employment and housing until the Hills returned. Beyond that I had no concrete plans. Pyongyang, once our country's Christian center and the missionaries' home away from home, was now a hotbed of hostility. Our school principal, a Christian, had already been expelled from Korea. Would missionaries be next? These were but a few of the unanswered questions that hopscotched across my mind as I walked through that blustery March evening.

Looking back over ten years at school, I realized that time doesn't stand still. It is as transitory as lightning crackling across the sky in a summer storm—here one instant and gone the next.

As I packed a few personal belongings the following morning, footsteps stopped at my door. It was Sinjune.

"I'll miss you, Chung Syn, and all the good times we've had." She squeezed my hand. "Mother and father are waiting in the lobby, but I couldn't leave without saying good-by. Be sure and write, and send your address."

"Of course, just as soon as I have one."

"Where are you going from here? To your parents?"

"Maybe. I'm not sure what the Lord has in store for me." At this point I'm confused."

"Why not sign the Shinto pledge and make things easier for yourself?"

"No, Sinjune. I can't pretend. It may be later than we think, and I want to make my time count for Christ."

She laid a restraining hand on my arm. "Please don't do anything reckless. You could be arrested . . . or worse."

"The police have more important people to arrest than a poor, blind girl," I assured her.

"Don't count on it. Besides . . ."

Our conversation was interrupted by the arrival of Moon and Soon-Cho. The latter was in tears.

"I'm betrothed," she wailed, "and the wedding is set for August. Father just told me. He's already signed the contract."

"And you don't like your fiancé?" I asked.

"I don't know him," she sobbed, blowing her nose before going on. "Father says he's a descendant of nobility, the grandson of Inn-suk Chul."

"Sounds impressive to me," Sinjune consoled. "If your father thinks he is a worthy son-in-law, you have nothing to worry about."

"But I don't want to get married . . . or live in Seoul with strangers." The ancient custom of professionally arranged marriages was gradually phasing out, but unfortunately not in time to prevent Soon-Cho from becoming an unwilling bride. I hoped her marriage, in spite of circumstances, would be a happy one.

True to their promise, the Hills "came home to Korea." How good it was to have them back! They were pleased when I told them I had not signed the Shinto pledge.

"If you don't have plans for the future," Mrs. Hill suggested, "why not stay with us for a while?"

I shook my head. "You have done enough already. It's time for me to be self-supporting."

Mrs. Hill knew me so well. "Something is bothering you, dear. What is it?"

"I'm concerned about Korea's future. Our people seem willing to take the course of least resistance."

"Few have your courage."

"It goes deeper than that. Without faith in God, many have nothing to cling to in times of trouble. Do you remember the opening lines of *Heike Monogatari?* It goes something like this: 'Temple bells echo the *impermanence* of all things. Even flowers testify to the truth that those who flourish must decay. For pride lasts but a little while, like dreams on a spring night. Before long even the mighty are cast down. They are dust before the wind.'"

Mrs. Hill sipped her tea a few seconds before answering. "Human nature hasn't changed. The world's philosophy is still 'eat, drink, and be merry, for tomorrow we die.' But Christians know they are more than 'dust before the wind.'"

"Yes, Christians have hope for tomorrow," I agreed.

"That is why we came to Korea in the first place, Chung Syn, to bring your people hope. Christ is the answer."

We sat in silence for a while before I found courage to share my nebulous plans. "A small Bible institute has just started near the outskirts of Pyongyang."

"Does it have government approval?"

"Probably not, but I would still like to enroll."

"And after that?"

"For years it has been my dream to go back to the country and teach God's Word in the farming community. Some settlements don't have churches or pastors. I would like to tell them about Jesus."

"The military police are keeping you under surveillance. This could be dangerous. Those scoundrels don't give up easily."

"I'm not afraid."

"But there are other things to consider—like your age and lack of experience."

"Have you forgotten that I've taught Sunday school classes since first going to middle school?"

"Filling the pulpit and teaching adults is quite another thing." Mrs. Hill covered my hand with hers as though to soften the impact of her words. "Your handicap will make the task even harder."

I nodded. "Everything you say is true, but for years I've been memorizing Scripture. Now I must share it."

"Have you considered the physical demands? Your health has never been good. Besides that, you can't travel alone."

I answered without hesitation. "If it is God's will, He will give me the strength and provide a companion."

"I concede," Mrs. Hill laughed. "You can count on us to help."

That afternoon her husband took me to the "campus"—an old house just outside the city—where I enrolled for Bible study. The accommodations were crude compared to the buildings at Soong-Yee and its well-cared-for campus, but students were congenial and all older than myself. We had one thing in common: a deep desire to tell our people about God's love and redeeming grace.

I studied at the makeshift institute until mid-June, reading and saturating my mind with Scripture. Little did I realize then that in the near future I would sit in a prison cell alone and recall many of those verses, one-by-one.

Mrs. Hyun, a fellow student, invited me to be the lay pastor at her home church. "We need someone young and enthusiastic to organize a children's program, as well as to fill the pulpit. I will gladly hire a guide, and you can stay in my home."

"Would your older members resent having a blind girl in their pulpit?"

"Of course not. They will love you, Chung Syn. Please come!"

I accepted the offer, and Rev. Hill took us to the train station the following morning. "This is a mighty big assignment for such a little lady, Chung Syn," he told me. "But I am convinced you can do the job. May God go with you."

On the train trip to Sinanju I learned more about my hostess. She was a widow of more than modest means, a very caring Christian with two daughters near my own age. Mrs. Hyun had built the Namchil church in her late husband's memory.

"My in-laws still have not forgiven me," she confided. I later learned Mrs. Hyun's in-laws were members of the Ahn clan and avidly anti-Christian. Several former pastors had left the church because of the family's violence—both actual and threatened.

Immediately I started teaching children's Bible classes. By

the end of that first week we had eighty sweet, cooperative, eager learners. I felt comfortable around these delightful youngsters, perhaps because I remembered my own joy when the "storylady" had told me about Jesus.

The first night I was to preach, however, my self-confidence fled quickly. As people gathered, I sat listening to the shuffling feet and hushed conversations. Doubts assailed me. If only I had something more suitable to wear than the tailored blouse, black skirt, and white rubber shoes of a middle-school student. The congregation could tell at a glance that I was still a teenager!

Curiosity finally got the better of me. I leaned over and asked Mrs. Hyun, "How many are here?"

"The church is almost full," she whispered in my ear. "People have traveled miles to see the blind, schoolgirl preacher."

Oh dear! Her words did nothing to bolster my courage, nor did the song service. Mrs. Hyun, the leader, sang off-key and made no attempt to follow tunes. I cringed and reminded myself that she was making a joyful noise unto the Lord.

Whatever their motives for coming, many went home that night and in the weeks to follow with minds and hearts touched by God. The Namchil church grew. Soon I was invited to speak to congregations at Yun-Dong, Poo-bek, and Songchil. Before long my companion and I were walking a circuit, regularly teaching hungry hearts the gospel.

During the monsoon season we sometimes waded through water chest-deep, hanging shoes around our necks and holding bundles over our heads. As the weeks passed I caught cold. A nagging cough lingered, and sleepless nights sapped my strength. Knowing that time was short and the needs many, I ignored these danger signals.

In several rural sections where superstitions and spiritual darkness had a strong hold, my companion and I met with

stiff opposition. On one occasion, when I had just stepped to
the pulpit, a disturbance developed outside the church. Dirt
clods spattered against the building; loud voices called out
curses and obscenities. Just as we bowed for prayer, a
windowpane shattered, and a well-aimed rock struck my
forehead, nearly knocking me off the platform. I struggled for
composure and raised my hand to quiet the congregation.

One of the hecklers, a young fellow who was no doubt under
the influence of *yak-ju,* staggered to the platform. Grabbing
my arm he spun me in a half-circle. "So the schoolgirl
preacher's brave, eh? Well . . . let's see how strong she is."
The upstart twisted my wrist, but I dodged as he attempted to
plant a kiss on my lips. In the ensuing struggle I somehow
managed to free myself.

"How dare you desecrate God's house!" I shouted angrily.

He moved closer. His hot breath steamed my face as he
sneered, "You're spunky . . . a little spitfire. Pretty too."

"Go away. Leave me alone," I screamed. As he lunged
toward me I pushed against his chest with both hands.
Already tipsy and then caught off guard, he toppled into the
front row—literally landing in the laps of several startled
women.

Although he didn't leave the service, the young man gave us
no more trouble that night. He stood utterly speechless, his
mouth gaping in amazement. Two weeks later Yung-mok
returned, quite sober and subdued. His wife said he hadn't
spoken a single word since that night he had accosted me in
the pulpit. She asked the congregation to pray for her
husband. We did, and his voice was restored. Later that
evening Yung-mok knelt at the altar and accepted Christ as
his Savior.

That was a wonderful summer! Not only did we see lives
transformed and church memberships grow but those weeks
gave me an opportunity to see God work *through* me—in spite

of my handicap and lack of experience. I also renewed my childhood love affair with the Korean countryside. While living in Pyongyang I had missed the mountains, the cool crisp air, and the simplicity of rural living.

My companion and I traveled along country lanes, walked in the woods, and sniffed the aroma of flowering acacias. Occasionally I helped Mrs. Hyun and her daughters gather tender mulberry leaves to feed their silkworms. Other times we went in search of wild berries.

These happy, carefree excursions lifted my spirit . . . and almost made me forget about the Shinto decree!

CHAPTER 14

A New Lease on Life

In September I conducted a series of meetings at Poo-bek. Afterward Mrs. Hyun suggested I come to her home for a rest.

"Chung Syn, I don't like the sound of that cough. You should see a doctor."

"Not now. Winter is closing in. Ice and snow will soon make these roads impassable. I'll rest later."

"Unless you die of pneumonia first," she chided. "You've been preaching and teaching for three months without a day off." Her voice softened. "I promised Mrs. Hill I'd look after you, remember?"

"Don't worry. I'm fine. Really! Besides, I've promised the children a special treat tomorrow for learning their memory verses. I can't disappoint them."

"Then let me teach your classes for a few days. Believe me," she laughed, "after one week, those youngsters will welcome you back with the 'Hallelujah Chorus'!"

I finally agreed. The persistent cough and pain in my chest had become more than a mere annoyance. Remembering the accusation of my former roommate, I was worried. Were her angry words a portent of things to come? Had I been carrying tuberculosis in a dormant stage all this time? Maybe I *should* see a physician!

I reluctantly returned to Sinanju with my hostess. She insisted on my going to bed immediately while she built a crackling fire in the *ondul* heater. Later Mrs. Hyun brought me a cup of steaming tea.

"Drink it, Chung Syn," she encouraged. "There's nothing better than a cup of *ginseng* to relieve a stuffy head." I didn't try and explain that it was my chest, not my head, that hurt. The bitter brew did infuse me with warmth. Soon, snuggled cozily in my *ibul*, I drifted into a fitful sleep.

Not until the following day did I realize how draining the past three months had been. For the better part of a week I remained in bed, hardly moving a muscle and dozing around the clock.

After I had regained some strength my hostess suggested we go for a walk: "It's beautiful outside. A stroll in the sunshine will be good for you."

Before we had reached the hilltop behind her home I was breathing heavily. Perspiration beaded on my forehead. My feet felt weighted with lead.

"Let's stop," I gasped.

Mrs. Hyun rested her hand on my arm. "What's wrong?"

"My chest." The effort of talking made me cough and gasp for air. Suddenly great gobs of something salty rose to my mouth. I stooped to clear my throat and nearly strangled.

"Chung Syn, you're coughing up blood!" Although spoken softly and with genuine concern those frightening words rang in my ears like a death knell. "Come to the house," she insisted, tugging on my arm as she spoke. "I'll send for a doctor."

Another fit of coughing left me weak and trembling. "No, I can't come back with you. It wouldn't be fair to the girls. Just pack my clothes. I'll wait here."

"Then what? Where will you go?"

"Back to Pyongyang. The train leaves at four."

"You can't travel alone . . . not in your condition. Let me come with you." I was too weak to protest. We both knew, though neither dared voice the suspicion, that my illness was more than a common cold.

With Mrs. Hyun carrying my things we walked to the depot, a distance of four miles, and arrived just as the locomotive screeched to a stop. During the train trip I sat by an open window, coughing up clots, chilling one instant and perspiring the next. At the Pyongyang station I started to hemorrhage again and lost considerable blood. Later, while slumped in the taxi my friend hailed, I drifted in and out of consciousness until we arrived at the Hill's.

"What happened?" my friends asked in unison. Their voices seemed to come from a great distance.

"I'm not certain, but Chung Syn needs a doctor. Fast!" Mrs. Hyun answered.

Turning to the taxi driver, Rev. Hill said, "Help me lift her into the back seat of my car."

The emergency room doctor took x-rays and gave me a complete examination. He called Rev. Hill aside, and I overheard parts of the conversation. Tuberculosis . . . advanced stage . . . massive hemorrhage . . . damaged lung tissue."

"What can we do?" Mrs. Hill gasped.

"Make her as comfortable as possible until there's an opening at Moranbong Sanitarium."

The Hills, unmindful of their own health, took me to their home until I could be moved to the tubercular facility.

Later, when there was room for me, Mrs. Hill drove me to the hospital. Patients such as myself were assigned to cottages, each equipped with a cot, dresser, toilet, and tiny kitchenette. As we approached my cottage Mrs. Hill exclaimed, "Chung

Syn, a lily is growing outside your door. Wonder who planted it there?" While helping me into bed she talked of trivialities in an effort to bolster my courage. But when time came for her to leave, I burst into uncontrollable sobs. Quickly she came back and gathered me into her arms.

"The doctor said . . . there's no hope." My words came haltingly and with great effort.

"Even doctors can be wrong," she hastened to say. "They are only human, you know. God performs miracles every day."

The nurse on duty was more professional than sympathetic. "Come now, this will never do," she chided. "Crying makes things worse. You must be brave."

I tossed and turned most of that night. Lying there alone, I felt as if the walls and ceiling were closing in, crushing my chest under a tremendous weight. I reached for a glass of water but was too weak to lift it. Any movement, even breathing, made my lungs burn as if seared by fire.

Days turned into weeks. One night as winds whistled through cracks in the reed door, I asked a maid to light my lamp before she went off duty.

"Why? What difference does it make? You can't see the light."

"I don't like being in the dark. Please light it," I insisted. The puzzled maid mumbled something under her breath. She obviously considered my request childish and ridiculous. How could I expect her to understand that the lamp's glow warmed and comforted me?

It wasn't unusual for my temperature to rise toward evening, but that night it soared. I tried to pray but had difficulty keeping my thoughts from wandering. Gradually I began to hallucinate, to hear footsteps and voices. Had someone come into the cottage without my knowing it?

"Who's there?" I called. No answer. I slipped out of bed

and walked about the room, my hands outstretched. The cottage seemed empty. Still fearful, I latched the reed door.

I am still not certain what happened that night. Some have said it was a dream, a state of delirium. Others have called it a vision. Whatever the explanation, I am convinced that God was with me. I sensed His divine presence by my bedside, felt the touch of His healing hand. An indescribable peace engulfed me. I was encouraged, infused with strength.

Next morning I awakened refreshed and with a new zest for life. My temperature had dropped drastically, and for the first time in months I felt ravenously hungry.

In my heart I knew that, psychologically at least, the biggest battle of my life had been won. "Though I walk through the valley of the shadow of death, I will fear no evil, for you are with me, your rod and your staff, they comfort me." I hadn't walked through the valley alone. My life—past, present, and future—was in the Good Shepherd's hands. I had nothing to fear!

When x-rays of my chest were taken again, they showed that the pulmonary lesions had completely healed! The following morning I walked out of Moranbong Sanitarium, a facility used exclusively for terminally ill patients, with the conviction that my recovery had been nothing short of a miracle. Doctors gave me a clean bill of health, but it was God who had given me a new lease on life.

I went to Sunbi's home in Song-wha to convalesce. How good it was to "see" her. We had a wonderful reunion, reminiscing until late every night. Being with my beloved sister again was more beneficial, healthwise, than all the medicine they had given me at the sanitarium—including the generous doses of cod-liver oil. (I still loathe the stuff!)

Spring came early that year. Soon the entire countryside was heavy with the sweet scent of peach blossoms. I was eager to get on with my life, and when Sunbi's husband started to prepare the soil for seedlings, I returned to Pyongyang.

For some time I had been concerned about the church I attended during my last years at school. Had the congregation scattered? My fears were confirmed! Political pressure had caused the Ha-cha-ri church's membership to drop from three hundred and fifty families to fifty-five. The struggling congregation invited me to be its pastor, and within three months attendance at the Sunday services had tripled.

I witnessed the goodness of God many times during my early years as an itinerant preacher and evangelist. What a thrill to see hearts and lives changed! When we held revival meetings at a small gold-mining town, an influential man, who for years had used his power to prevent the spread of Christianity, came to Christ. The entire community rejoiced! During another meeting a demented woman's mind was restored. As a result her entire family accepted the Lord.

In December of 1939 a sudden and serious epidemic of measles spread like fire from village to village. Thirteen children from our congregation died at the onset and scores of others were afflicted within a few days. I felt so helpless! What could I do without training or medical supplies? I went from home to home comforting the bereaved and doing as much as possible for the stricken families, praying with them, staying with them, and giving my moral support.

During the epidemic I developed an excruciating pain in my side. It came and went from time to time, and not until my stomach started to swell did I become alarmed and resolve to see a doctor at the first opportunity. Before I carried out that resolution, however, a special messenger delivered an official letter to the Ha-cha-ri church. It came from the police and was addressed to Miss Chung Syn Yang.

I cringed as a sighted member of the congregation read the threatening message aloud.

CHAPTER 15

Land of the Rising Sun

The police notice came as no surprise. Classmates had discouraged me from carrying the torch for Christ, and others had repeatedly warned me that a day of reckoning would come. Father, discouraged and disillusioned, felt it foolish for me to endanger my life by preaching.

"Why crusade for a lost cause?" he asked. "You are flirting with danger, Chung Syn. Forget this nonsense . . . and come home." Father spoke from experience, and he was a logical man. Why waste time trying to convince him that this was something I *must* do, regardless of personal safety? He would never understand.

For two years I had been preaching and teaching, traveling from place to place unnoticed and unmolested by occupation forces. Now that authorities knew of my activities would they arrest me? Should I surrender? Or leave? No doubt I would be safer at Song-wha but the measles' epidemic had not yet peaked; many were still ill. Since my congregation needed me I chose to stay with them, come what may.

Another threatening letter followed the first one. I ignored them both. After the third warning, however, I felt it would be wise to make a personal appearance. Since the pain in my side persisted I walked to the police department with a bandage supporting my swollen stomach.

A Korean officer was in charge of the precinct office. He greeted me with pseudo-politeness and spoke in our native tongue. "So you finally decided to make an appearance, Miss Yang?" he asked. "How nice of you to come." The words were tinged with sarcasm.

"Why did you send for me, sir?" I inquired, ignoring his condescending comment. "What are the charges?"

Instantly he switched to the Japanese language. "You have failed to sign the Shinto pledge of faith," he boomed, his voice raised in anger. "Furthermore, you have flagrantly spread lies among our people. By preaching this kind of propaganda you have defied the Governor General."

"They are not lies, sir, nor propaganda. I only teach the Word of God."

"Bah!" he snorted. "You are a traitor and an infidel! You have scorned Shinto . . . and the Emperor of Japan. I shall report you to higher authorities."

"Do it if you must, sir . . . but please allow me to see a doctor first. I may have appendicitis."

Begrudgingly he agreed to let me check in at Kitok. (Even the hospital at this juncture was more appealing than jail!) Doctors diagnosed my problem as peritonitis and performed immediate surgery. During my convalescence officers from the police precinct came to check on me regularly. It appeared that my arrest was imminent.

"Chung Syn, you must leave Korea at once," Rev. Hill finally warned.

"But . . . where could I go?"

"You've always wanted to study voice. The Municipal School of Music at Osaka, I'm told, is one of the finest."

His words were sobering. "Are you suggesting that I study voice . . . in Japan?"

"Why not? The idea isn't as dangerous as it may sound. You would actually be safer there than here right now."

"How could I possibly go to Japan alone? Besides . . . it would take a fortune. Thanks for the suggestion, but there's no way I could come up with that kind of money."

"Don't worry about finances. Mary and I have already agreed to give you a year's scholarship. There's only one thing that stands in the way. You may have trouble getting a passport on short notice."

"H-m-m-m," I mused, warming up to the idea in spite of myself. "Wonder if Uncle Inn-suk could help? He's quite an influential man in Pyongyang, though father hasn't seen him in several years." In reality the two brothers weren't even on speaking terms. According to father, Uncle Inn-suk was an unscrupulous scoundrel who had absconded with family funds—money from the sale of father's pepper crop. The sum was sizable, enough to take him to Japan. While there he attended school and gained favor with the enemy. Now Uncle Inn-suk was back home, consorting with occupation forces and enjoying a position of prestige in Korea. It was rumored that he lived lavishly and entertained Japanese dignitaries in an impressive three-story home.

I went to see Uncle Inn-suk the day doctors discharged me from the hospital. "What brings you here?" he asked, seemingly surprised by a visit from his blind niece.

"I am in a bit of trouble . . . with the police."

"Speak up! What have you done, Chung Syn?"

I braced myself for a scathing rebuke and squared my shoulders. "I refused to sign the Shinto pledge. That is all."

"You're a foolish girl," he snorted, "as stubborn as my brother Sihwal. Sign the pledge! Why make trouble for yourself?"

"I am a Christian, Uncle Inn-suk."

"So?"

"So I can't sign the pledge or worship at Shinto shrines."

Uncle Inn-suk struck a match and puffed on his pipe before answering. "The trouble with you, my girl, is that you refuse to keep pace with the times. One doesn't get ahead in this world by being stubborn. Take me and my brother for example. I made friends with the Japanese," he boasted, "and see what it got me—a beautiful home with servants. While I live comfortably in the city, your father works hard . . . and his family lives in poverty. Sometimes," he smirked, "it pays to bend a bit . . . like a willow in the breeze."

I thought it wisest to ignore his insinuating remark and resort to flattery. "Uncle, you are a successful man, and very influential. I want to go to Japan and study music. Maybe I can be successful too. Could you help me get a passport?"

"Now you're talking sense," he chortled, slapping his leg with obvious delight. "To make friends with the lion one goes to his lair. Right?" I nodded half-heartedly and forced a smile. "You've got spunk, Chung Syn. I like that! Come back in the morning. In the meantime I'll try to get your passport."

By pulling political strings Uncle Inn-suk obtained a credential for me to leave Korea, and in record time everything else was arranged for an early departure. Rev. Hill booked passage for me on a ship sailing from Pusan. He and his dear wife also gave me four hundred *won* to cover tuition and traveling expenses; that same evening Yu-nok, who was now a student in the capital, took me to the depot.

It all happened so quickly! Before authorities knew what was going on, and before there was time for me to change my mind, I was on a train speeding toward the coast. My greatest concern was making connections in Pusan. How would I get from the train to the ship? Providentially that detail was taken care of enroute.

A porter paged my name. "Miss Yang?"

"Yes, sir."

"A message just arrived from Mr. Lee. He will meet you in Seoul. You are to wait for him at the depot." I heaved a sigh of relief. How did my friend from the blind school know that I needed a guide?

"Thank you, Lord," I whispered softly.

"What did you say?" the porter asked, coming back to my seat.

I handed him a tip. "Thank you, sir, for the message."

Mr. Lee accompanied me from Seoul to Pusan and even came on board to help me get oriented before sailing. Only after he had gone ashore did I begin having qualms about leaving everything near and dear to me. How could I cope with foreign living conditions without a companion? Was this a hasty, ill-advised venture? Should I forget the whole thing? But the decision had been made. At that instant the throb of pulsating engines reached my ears. For a split second the ship seemed to shudder and strain at its mooring. Then, like a bird on the wing, it gracefully glided into the night.

We were on our way to Japan!

Many have asked me why a young woman of twenty— handicapped, alone, and vulnerable under the most favorable conditions—would voluntarily move into hostile territory.

In reality there were several influencing factors. Japan's doors had long been open to missionaries, and Christianity had gained a firm foothold. Ironically Christians still had more freedom of worship there than in occupied Korea.

Another enticement was the generous four hundred-*won* scholarship that I hoped would enable me to study voice under some of the finest instructors in the Orient. This unexpected opportunity thrilled me beyond words.

Being young and adventuresome by nature, I also had a yen

to travel, to experience firsthand the world I had only read about in books.

The clinching factor, of course, was political pressure back home. I hoped that by dropping out of sight for a year my former transgressions would be forgotten, if not forgiven.

During that night, choppy water and high winds buffeted the small boat, bouncing it from one wave to the next like an empty *yak-ju* bottle. By morning my stomach felt a trifle squeamish, and, as the sturdy little ship approached Shimonoseki harbor, I struggled to keep my footing on the unpredictable deck. A fine spray made the wood planks slippery and treacherous, so I decided to wait for the other passengers to disembark. Eager to get ashore, they impatiently pushed toward the gangplank. I stepped back to let them pass but found myself being carried along by the crowd—involuntarily. It was too late to turn back!

Thus on a cold March day in 1940, I first set foot in Japan. My pulse pounded with excitement, but as I stood there, alone in the crowd and wondering what to do next an inexplicable feeling of foreboding came over me. Again I wondered if I had made an impulsive, foolish move. Would Japanese students resent having a handicapped Korean in their midst?

As these thoughts raced through my mind, I overheard another traveler, also from Korea, ask a Japanese policeman for directions. Neither could speak or understand the other's language, and they were having a difficult time trying to communicate. Hesitantly I approached them.

"Pardon me, please. I didn't mean to eavesdrop, but perhaps I can translate for you." The frustrated woman seemed greatly relieved to find someone from home, and noticing the white cane in my hand she volunteered to be my guide until time for our train. After several hours of sight-seeing we went to a nice hotel and had dinner together before boarding the Tokyo Express.

Enroute to Osaka I made the acquaintance of a young Japanese student. He was a friendly fellow and spoke of the school I hoped to attend in glowing terms. When the train arrived at our destination he insisted on carrying my luggage, even called a cab that took me straight to the school.

Since I had left Korea on the spur of the moment there hadn't been time to make a formal application. I was trusting the Lord to intercede on my behalf—and He did. Mr. Kanezawa waived the customary formalities and agreed to give me an audition first thing the next morning.

"You have a lovely voice, Miss Yang," he said after finishing the audition. "With training and practice you will become a fine lyric soprano. Classes start on April 10th."

"You mean . . . I am accepted?"

"Yes. It will be a pleasure to have you in our school, and I hope you will be happy here. If there is anything you need please let me know." I bowed in the Japanese tradition and thanked him for his kindness. In a matter of minutes the interview was over.

A maid took me to my room. It was small and sparsely furnished, for here in Japan people practiced floor-level-living. Instead of sitting on chairs they knelt on cushions. At night comforters were spread on straw *dadami* mats for sleeping, then folded and stored in cabinets during the day. Low *chow* tables sufficed for both desk work and dining. Folding *shoji* screens, sometimes elaborately carved of teakwood and covered with translucent rice paper, provided a bit of privacy and served as room dividers.

In only a few minutes I had unpacked my meager possessions. After getting settled I knelt before the small table and Brailled a letter to Rev. and Mrs. Hill. "Thank you for your prayers," I wrote. "They have been answered! God has met every need, and I am now a student at the Osaka Municipal School of Music. You will never know how grateful

I am to you both for giving me this wonderful opportunity. Thank you from the bottom of my heart."

At tea time that day I met several other students and a number of instructors. They cordially accepted me and endeavored to make me feel comfortable and at ease.

At dinner I was first introduced to Japanese cuisine. The meal included fish, sliced and served raw with a hot, peppery soy sauce. Since seafood, no matter how it was camouflaged, had never been to my liking, I ate only boiled rice, soybean curd, and vegetables. Later I learned to avoid some of the cook's other specialties—dishes concocted of squid, eel, seaweed, and shellfish of all kinds. The unmistakable aroma of fish invariably brought back unpleasant memories of cod-liver oil!

That weekend, Uri Awakawa, a fellow voice student, took me by trolley to the city park. Together we strolled over quaint little bridges that spanned fountains, waterfalls, and goldfish ponds. She described the gravel gardens that were raked into artistic designs, and I tried to visualize the word pictures she painted. Uri explained that Japanese gardens are an expression of poetry, philosophy, and art. How I yearned to see them.

"Are the cherry trees in blossom?" I asked.

"Yes, they've just begun to bud. Later this month they will be in full bloom. Do you have cherry trees in Korea?"

"Oh yes. I remember *seeing* them as a child."

That year the annual music festival was being held in Osaka. I could feel excitement mounting as students practiced for the traditional competition.

"Why don't you enter the solo division, Chung Syn?" Uri asked one morning after we had finished rehearsing a choir number. "Who knows? You might win a blue ribbon."

"Little chance," I laughed. "Besides, singing a solo before a crowd would scare me half-to-death."

"All the more reason you should enter," she insisted. "We've both got to do it sooner or later, you know. Why not now?"

My voice teacher was equally insistent.

I tried to make excuses. "But I've never competed before. There isn't time to learn a new number, and I don't have a pretty kimono to wear."

"Don't worry about a costume. I'll loan you one. Just be yourself, and sing something simple."

That was easier said than done! I *did* worry! What should I sing? Would I look stupid—carrying a white cane while wearing a floor length kimono with a butterfly *obi* sash? What if I stumbled?

I needn't have worried. When my turn came to step on stage someone led me to the microphone and left me standing there alone. My trembling fingers reached out and grasped the music stand for support. My heart pounded furiously. Knowing that eyes were focused on my face I forced a smile and tried to relax while waiting for the accompaniment to start. My throat was dry, but after the first chord sounded I found myself singing with confidence. The words flowed smoothly, softly at first and then building into a final crescendo. Moments later I walked off the stage with resounding applause ringing in my ears.

No one was more surprised than I when the awards were announced. "And now, ladies and gentlemen," the master of ceremonies began, "first place in the soprano solo division goes to a student from the Osaka Municipal School of Music . . . Miss Chung Syn Yang. Please join me in giving her a hand."

I nearly fainted from shock!

CHAPTER 16

From Music
to Medicine

Everything at school—social activities, dorm life, and dining room conversations—revolved around music. I thoroughly enjoyed being a student again. Living expenses, however, were draining my bank account. In addition to instrumental fees, there were books to buy, costumes to rent, and costly musical scores to purchase. At this rate my money would be gone before the first semester ended. What then?

During my brief stay in Osaka I had made numerous acquaintances, but none had developed into meaningful friendships or showed any such promise. Except for music, I had little in common with the other students. They were all Japanese by birth, sighted, and of the Shinto faith. Although no one referred to my nationality or faith in a derogatory manner, it was impossible to forget that I was indeed a stranger in a strange land. I didn't really belong.

Mary and Harry Hill had expected their four hundred *won* would last a full year, not realizing how costly the course would be. I didn't feel inclined to write home and ask for more money; my American friends had done too much already.

Instead I talked my financial situation over with Mr. Kanezawa.

"It would be most unfortunate for you to leave school because of a lack of funds," he said. "What can we do to help?"

"Sir, I thought perhaps you could suggest a way for me to supplement my income."

He was silent for a few seconds, apparently searching his mind for a solution. Finally he asked, "Would you be willing to take a part-time job?"

"Of course, sir. I have always worked, at one thing or another."

"What would you like to do?"

"I attended a school for the blind in Pyongyang where they taught massage. My hands are very strong, and my instructor said I would make a good masseuse."

"H-m-m-m. I have a friend who is affiliated with a hospital. Let me call him and see if there is an opening in physical therapy."

The dean's friend was director of Misima School of Medicine (now affiliated with Osaka University). My initial interview with this busy man was a short cryptic encounter in Mr. Kanezawa's office. After a brief exchange of questions and answers he offered me an opportunity to work a few hours daily in the physical therapy department at the medical school's hospital. I suspected the gesture was made out of sympathy and a desire to accommodate his old friend, but whatever his motivation I accepted with gratitude. This meant I could continue my pursuit of music.

The hospital fascinated me! It didn't take long to learn the hospital routine, the new techniques, and how to use the latest equipment. Because of blindness I had developed strong hands and unusual sensitivity in my fingertips, both of which helped in giving treatments. Acupuncture, the ancient oriental practice of inserting needles near nerve centers to relieve pain and treat various ailments, intrigued me. Every hour spent at the hospital was pure pleasure. I listened and learned as much as possible and as time went on spent more hours there asking questions than at the music conservatory vocalizing.

One day Dr. Okawa summoned me to his office. The director was an older gentleman, all business and not prone to wasting time on trivialities. "Miss Yang, I like your work," he announced, speaking in short, staccato tones. "You impress me as being a brilliant young woman."

"Thank you, doctor. Thank you very much," I stammered.

"How would you like to study medicine instead of music?" What a sobering thought. "But, sir, I am blind."

His voice softened. "I know. But you haven't answered my question. Are you interested in taking a medical course?"

Memories of the measles' epidemic flashed before me—standing beside grieving parents as their children died without medical attention. Then, and many times since, I had longed for the skills that would enable me to serve the Lord more effectively. Was this, perhaps, the reason God had brought me to Japan?

"Sir, doctors are desperately needed in Korea. Nothing would make me happier than learning the skills of your profession. But I hear that even color-blind students aren't admitted to medical school."

"That is true."

"Then why would you suggest. . . ?"

"Because you have an inquisitive mind. Already you are an excellent masseuse, and I believe you would be a credit to our profession. I understand you learned to thread needles."

My face flushed. "Yes, sir. How did you know?"

Dr. Okawa chuckled in a most ingratiating way. "Word travels fast, Miss Yang." Despite his professionalism and brusque manner Misima's director was extremely warm and compassionate. Nothing escaped his notice. "It seems only logical that anyone who could accomplish such a difficult feat, in spite of handicaps, would make a fine physician. Have you had the basic science and math classes?" I nodded. Immediately he began probing my knowledge of chemistry, biology, physiology, algebra, and physics, firing questions at me with the rapidity of an expert marksman. "I am convinced you have the necessary background. The final decision is yours. Classes start immediately."

I was still uncertain. "Doctor, your offer is most generous . . . and very tempting. But what if I can't keep up? All of my notes have to be taken in Braille, which is much slower than regular writing. Exams would be another problem. I can't read questions on the blackboard. Someone would have to read them aloud."

"That could be arranged. However, I must warn you that some doctors on staff are skeptical. It will, in the final analysis, be up to you to prove that the scoffers are wrong." He paused. "If you succeed, after a year's probation, you have a full, four-year scholarship."

"I am ready to try, sir."

As he escorted me to the door Dr. Okawa said, "When you have lived as many years as I have, you will discover that there are two kinds of people: those who sit by the water's edge and wait for the current to bring their ship of fortune into port, and those who aren't afraid to plunge in and swim out to meet it. I can see that you are a swimmer!"

I shall never forget my first bewildering day as a medical student. From an atmosphere that centered on individual talent, expression, and aesthetic presentation, I had stepped into a world of hard, cold, scientific facts in which there was no room for variables. At Misima everyone concentrated on precision and exactitude. For me the transition seemed confusing.

After that first anatomy class was dismissed I stayed in my seat, hoping to ask Professor Okumura some pertinent questions about the assignment he had written on the blackboard. I heard footsteps. They stopped beside my desk.

"*Ohaiyo gozaimas*" (Good morning), a deep masculine voice greeted. "My name is Sinbo. What is yours?"

"Chung Syn . . . Chung Syn Yang," I responded.

"From Korea, right?" I nodded. "How do you like living in Japan?" This young student was completely uninhibited, an unusual quality. Most strangers found it difficult to relate to a blind person in the beginning, but Sinbo seemed quite at ease. I liked his frankness.

"In many respects Japan is quite similar to my own country," I responded. "Everyone has been kind and helpful."

"You came here just to study medicine?"

"Not really. At first I was enrolled in a music course."

He seemed puzzled. "Then what are you doing at Misima?"

I smiled. "It's a long story. Dr. Okawa encouraged me to switch. Now I'm wondering if it was wise. Do your professors always talk so fast? I'm having trouble taking notes."

Sinbo sat down and opened his notebook. "What did you miss? Maybe I can help." He answered each question in detail before reading the assignment, pausing occasionally to let me take it down in Braille. I thanked him, and we parted.

Next day I was pleasantly surprised when this same young man sat in an empty seat beside me. Several times during the lecture he leaned over and explained some puzzling point. The resonance of his voice sent shivers down my spine, and each time our hands accidently touched my heart began to flutter. *Why?*

After class Sinbo asked, "Are you free this afternoon?"

"I'll be giving treatments at the hospital until three."

"Then why don't we study together this evening?" When I

hesitated he hastened to add, "Unless there is someone else you would rather study with." His voice sounded eager.

"No," I assured him, "there is no one else. In fact, you are an answer to prayer."

"Really?" he enthused. "Then you must be a Christian. So am I!"

Little did I realize then that Sinbo—Japanese by birth but Christian by faith—would become the most influential, helpful, and unforgettable man in my life! From then on we sat together in classes and spent much of our free time comparing notes and studying. When I needed encouragement he was there to spur me on; and several times he kept me from giving up. Sinbo became my eyes. Without his help and understanding that anatomy class would surely have ended in disaster.

The first time Professor Okumura dissected a cadaver in class I was lost in the shuffle. Being unable to see the demonstration, nothing he said made sense. I couldn't visualize the organs themselves or picture their relative positions in the body. Again, Sinbo came to my rescue. After the others left the lab he encouraged me to touch the specimen and explore the cavity with my fingertips. Instinctively I recoiled, but he gently guided my hands from one organ to the next. Evenings we sometimes returned to the lab so I could feel life-sized models and familiarize myself with bone structure as well as muscles. Thanks to Sinbo I passed the course!

Strangely enough my most frustrating challenge came when we started the study of amphibians. Remembering it brings back a smile, even now. An assistant filled the lab pond with frogs. We were each to skin one of the slippery little creatures and record pertinent physiological data. For three days I struggled unsuccessfully with the project. Each slippery frog I caught managed to slither through my fingers and jump around the lab floor—with me in helpless pursuit. It must have been hilarious to watch for the entire class snickered. Everyone, that is, but Sinbo. He came to stand behind me.

"I can't do it, Sinbo. It's impossible," I whispered, struggling for composure. Tears of humiliation trickled down my cheeks.

He leaned over my shoulder and answered softly. "Yes you can, Chung Syn. Nothing is impossible . . . for a Christian."

His words fell on deaf ears. I hurried to my room and started packing. *That does it!* I fumed. *Let them laugh at someone else for a change. It was stupid to come here in the first place. I'll never set foot in that lab again. Never!*

Next morning Sinbo spotted me walking across campus toward the administration building. "Where are you going?" he asked.

"Home . . . just as soon as I can check out!"

Sinbo knew when to be forceful, when to be gentle. He fell into step by my side and slowly steered me toward the lab. "You are going to class, Chung Syn. Now . . . with me! *Ka-e-roo ni makete ka-e-roo-ka?*" he asked. In Japanese the word *ka-e-roo* can be used as a verb meaning "to go home," or as a noun meaning "frog." *Was I going home because of a frog?* He had used a clever play on words to show me how foolish a defeatist attitude is.

I smiled in spite of myself and walked willingly at his side. "Thank you. You are right. Guess I was only feeling sorry for myself."

After class I cleared a lab table for action, netted an unwilling frog, and with an injection needle and scalpel in hand started trying to pin and dissect my specimen. Perhaps *butcher* would be a more accurate description. Sinbo, understanding my independent spirit, watched in silence until I asked for help. Then he guided my fingers, patiently explaining how to skin an amphibian skillfully, later removing the air sac and entrails to expose its vital organs. I practiced over and over again, practically depleting the lab's supply of frogs. When our projects were due I could dissect a specimen to the professor's satisfaction, and the entire class gathered around to watch me do it. This time no one snickered!

My next big hurdle was bacteriology. Other classes that involved memorizing material were relatively simple, but, in this one, sight was very important. Since I couldn't use a microscope or see pictures to identify the organisms we were studying, Sinbo devised a clever means of helping me learn their shapes by touch. He did the microscopic research for both of us then carefully drew a diagram of each organism, using my stylus to make the raised outlines. By touching the dots I could visualize their shapes and duplicate them for the professor when it came time for examinations. Thanks to Sinbo's ingenuity I passed that course also!

One evening while I studied in my room a Brailled note fell out of my textbook. Sinbo had put it there earlier in the day. It wasn't the note's content that thrilled me half as much as the fact that somewhere my friend had learned the Braille alphabet.

Next morning we met before class, as was our custom. "I found your note, Sinbo."

"Oh? Did you like it?" he asked.

I smiled at his boyishness. "Of course . . . but I'm puzzled."

"What about?"

"Who taught you the Braille alphabet?"

Sinbo laughed and answered smugly, "No one. I learned it by watching you."

Sinbo's patience and imagination never ceased to amaze me—nor did the depth of his devotion!

CHAPTER 17

Budding Love

As time went on Sinbo and I discovered many things in common besides our mutual involvement in medicine. As enthusiastic young adults eager to live life to the fullest, we spent many leisure hours together, and each exciting thing we shared seemed to strengthen and deepen the bonds of our relationship.

By the end of my second semester at Misima, Sinbo and I were close, caring companions. We discussed many things—the challenges and rewards of a medical career, our mutual love for the Lord, and our desire to serve Him in the future. Sinbo, like myself, was a curious composite of idealist and scientist. His lofty ambition was to serve God as a Christian physician somewhere in Japan. My desire was to do the same thing—in Korea!

From the beginning of our relationship, Sinbo seemed to anticipate my needs before they were even voiced. In addition to completing his own assignments on time he was usually on hand to help me over the hurdles when I needed him most. Every day I thanked God for sending Sinbo into my life!

Between semesters I visited the Tanima church where
Sinbo and his family attended Sunday services. His mother
was genuinely gracious, as generous and thoughtful as her
son. She invited me to their home for dinner and carefully
avoided the subject of my handicap and nationality. I couldn't
help wonder how she really felt about her son's friendship with
a blind Korean. Would she rather have him court a sighted,
Japanese girl, someone with a similar background? If so she
kept such thoughts to herself.

Many of our classmates were not so magnanimous. They
resented the fact that Sinbo was devoting so much time to a
handicapped outsider. Even his friends disapproved and gave
him a rough time, at first by innuendo and then through snide
remarks. Some even made unkind comments in my presence
about him courting a *mekura kaikokuyin* (blind foreigner).
Perhaps such a reaction was inevitable since I came from a
country under Japanese occupation, nonetheless it hurt to
know that Sinbo was being ridiculed because of me.

Realizing that my nationality and lack of sight would
always be a barrier between us—at least in the minds of
others—I tried to avoid Sinbo. He refused to be discouraged
and if anything became more attentive. Finally I decided to
candidly discuss the gossip that was circulating across
campus.

"Maybe we should stop seeing so much of each other, at
least for a while."

"Why?" he asked. "Are you tired of having a shadow?" He
tried to sound nonchalant, but I detected disappointment in
his voice.

"Of course not. It's just that people are talking."

"Let them. Why should we care?"

"I don't want you to be hurt because of me. You deserve the
best, Sinbo, a pretty Japanese girl you can be proud of . . .
someone who can *see*."

Sinbo reached for my hand and covered it with both of his. "I am proud of *you* . . . very proud. Remember 'Beauty is in the eyes of the beholder.' I have never known anyone with your kind of beauty. It is something special that comes from the Lord." He squeezed my hand ever so gently before releasing it. "Just being with you makes me happy, Chung Syn. Doesn't that count for something?" I merely nodded, too choked with emotion to answer. No one had ever spoken to me in this way before!

Several days later as I left the dorm Sinbo grabbed my arm. "I am being sent on assignment to a military hospital in Tokyo . . . right away."

"But why? I don't understand."

"Rumor says that Japan has suffered some stinging losses, that hospitals are overflowing with military casualties. There will undoubtedly be many more before the war is over.

I knew how deeply Sinbo felt about the current conflicts in Europe and his own country's conquests in eastern Asia. Being a peaceful man he loathed violence of any kind. "I'm ashamed of the way your people have been mistreated," he comforted. "And if my country needs me I'll serve in the medical corps—not as a soldier. I want to ease suffering . . . not cause it."

Even I was to become involved, like it or not. Shortly after Sinbo left Osaka my own assignment came, and we didn't meet again for several weeks. Miss Hujida, a senior student, accompanied me to the Tamba District Hospital where we helped nurse wounded soldiers and comfort their families. This, my first intimate exposure to war casualties, was a sobering experience. We ate and slept at a school along with other volunteers, remaining there for three weeks before being transferred to the Minami Army Hospital in Kyoto.

In spite of a busy and exhaustive summer schedule I found myself thinking of Sinbo more and more frequently. I missed him dreadfully and looked forward to the time when we could be together again. Memories of him made my pulse quicken and my heart turn flips.

We both returned to the Misima campus in early August to begin the fall semester. "Oh, Chung Syn, I thought the summer would never end!" Sinbo greeted me.

I shyly agreed.

New classes presented new challenges. We rarely had a free moment to discuss newspaper headlines or worsening world conditions. Because of the national food shortage, however, civilian rations had been drastically cut, and we were feeling the pinch on campus. Each day the school menu shrank. Since my work schedule at the hospital varied I sometimes missed meals altogether.

Dean Kanezawa, who had kept in close contact with me since my switch from music to medicine, suggested that I rent a housekeeping room. "Friends of mine have a vacancy in the back of their home that's clean and comfortable. It has a kitchenette with running water and a gas burner where you could prepare your own meals. I'll take you to see about it." The small room met all the necessary requirements and was even near a trolley stop. That same afternoon the dean helped me move in.

On August 22nd I returned to my new home after school and found two policemen waiting to question me. "You are an alien?"

I nodded.

"What is your name? Nationality? Why are you in Japan? What is your father's name and occupation?"

I answered their queries honestly and without hesitation, thinking such questions merely routine. After they left I dismissed the incident from my mind entirely—until several weeks later.

I enjoyed living alone. The dorm had been noisy. Here it

was quiet, and I could study as late as I liked. Shopping for food, cooking my own meals, and commuting by trolley, however, were time-consuming.

On the afternoon of December 7, 1941, a date I shall never forget, Sinbo rushed into the chemistry lab where I was running some tests.

"Have you heard the news?" he asked excitedly.

"No. What's happened?"

"Our air force attacked Pearl Harbor this morning!"

"You mean . . . Japan and the United States are at war?"

"Yes. The radio announcer said several U.S. battleships have already been sunk."

My knees started to shake, and I dropped into the nearest chair. Sinbo came to kneel beside me. "Are you ill?" he asked.

"No. I'm worried about the Hills. Do you think they'll be arrested . . . or sent home?"

"It's anybody's guess. We need to pray that God will protect them. I doubt that mail will get through." Neither of us realized that my own safety was also in jeopardy—or that soon I would learn firsthand about the inhumanities of war.

Sinbo was on a field trip the night my ordeal began. Feeling in need of spiritual refreshment I attended services at the Kobe United Church, returning to my small apartment alone. A few moments later a knock sounded at the door. I opened it and was confronted by a pair of burly policemen.

"Step aside," they ordered. "We are here to search the premises." Puzzled and terribly frightened, I stood in a corner as they went through all my belongings—including Braille books, personal papers, and official documents from Korea. Finally one found a stack of letters and several pictures that had been sent to me by American missionaries. He waved them before my face and accused me of having connections with the enemy. I protested, but nothing I said convinced him.

"You are under arrest!" he shouted. "Your father was a traitor, an enemy of Japan. So are you!" They slipped handcuffs on my wrists and literally whisked me from the room empty-handed, without even a toothbrush.

My landlady, as frightened as I, stood in the hall as we passed. "Chung Syn," she wailed. "What can I do?"

"Call Dr. Okawa! Ask him . . . to get in touch with Sinbo." They dragged me away before I could say anything more.

At the police station I was fingerprinted and booked. My heart beat so furiously that it was difficult to control my voice and answer their questions. As I stood there, trembling from head to foot, I silently repeated Psalm 56:3 to myself—over and over again: "When I am afraid, I will trust in you." It helped! Gradually my fears subsided, and my pulse stopped pounding.

After a few moments another officer led me to a tiny, unheated cell that I was to share with bedbugs, cockroaches, and lice! I later discovered a latrine in one corner, a filthy pallet in the other, nothing else. The cubicle apparently had no windows, for its stagnant air reeked with vile odors, including the stench of urine. I found it nauseating and gagged as the officer pushed me inside, slamming the cell door behind him.

When the sound of his echoing footsteps faded into the distance I dropped to my knees on the dirty pallet and prayed, not only for God's protection, but for *peace that passes all understanding*. My heart was filled with fear and foreboding. I needed peace of mind that only He could give.

That first night I slept very little. I had no blankets and they had hustled me away from home without a coat or wrap of any kind. For hours I lay awake, shivering and frightened by noises which intermittently drifted through the iron bars. Did that piercing scream come from the interrogation room? Or was it just another prisoner having nightmares?

Something cold crawled across my face! A cockroach? I frantically brushed it off and jumped to my feet. For the rest of that night I paced the floor—six steps forward, and six steps back. The same unanswered questions raced through my mind. *Why did they arrest me? How long will I be kept here? Does Dr. Okawa have political influence, enough to get me released?* First and foremost in my thoughts was Sinbo. *Would I ever hear the sound of his familiar voice again?*

In the midst of my confused and chaotic thoughts came words once spoken by Isaiah: "You will keep in perfect peace him whose mind is steadfast, because he trusts in you. Trust in the LORD forever, for the LORD, the LORD is the Rock eternal" (26:3–4). If ever I needed strength it was now!

Toward morning the echo of clicking boots resounded in the corridor. I crouched in the corner as those footsteps came closer. Finally they stopped. Icy fingers gripped my heart when a noisy key grated in the lock. I waited expectantly, hoping and praying the jailor had come to tell me there had been a terrible mistake, that I was now free to leave. Instead the unseen visitor stepped inside and yanked me to my feet.

"Gomen nasai, Jo" (Excuse me, Miss), a mocking voice sneered. "It's time for your trial." Actually formal charges were never filed. Nor did the courts give me a hearing. Instead I was taken directly to the interrogation room and subjected to the most depraved and degrading forms of humiliation. My interrogators were bigoted and brutal. They accused me of being a *gunji tantei* (spy) for the United States and of working with my father in the Korean underground. I denied their accusations—but to no avail.

"You lie!" they railed. "We received a full report from the Pyongyang Police. They told us what you are up to, so don't deny it. Who are these Americans? What have you told them about Japan?"

I could divulge no military secrets. I knew none! But they

wouldn't believe me. "I am not a spy! The pictures you found in my room are of missionaries—the kind people who are helping me through school."

"Another lie!" one sneered.

I tried to reason with them. "How could a blind woman be a spy? I am a student at the Misima medical school. Nothing more. You can check my credentials with Dr. Okawa."

"Then why do you keep coded messages in your room?" He shoved a sheet of Brailled chemical formulas into my hand. "Try and explain these away . . . if you can."

"Have you never seen Braille before? These are only classroom notes." I was so nervous that the sheet of paper accidentally slipped through my fingers and fluttered to the floor.

"Pick it up!" he ordered, his voice raised in anger. Before I had time to comply someone slapped my face with a force that made me stagger and slump to the floor.

"Answer my questions," the interrogator snapped. "Tell us what we need to know. Who are you working with? How many agents are in Japan? Who is your contact in Osaka?"

"No one! I'm not a spy. Please believe me," I sobbed, trying to crawl away from the sound of his voice.

"Your underground is clever . . . but not clever enough. Hiding behind the skirts of a blind woman won't work."

"Call Dr. Okawa. He will tell you I am not a spy."

"You are lying again," he shouted. His voice sounded menacing. "But we have ways of making you tell the truth. Don't we men?"

The others laughed. "Yeah," one agreed. "She sure is a pretty little thing. Too bad she's blind."

As I struggled to my feet the officer in charge moved closer. His hot breath on my face smelled of *sake*. Instinctively I backed away, but immediately he grabbed my arm in a viselike grip and yanked me toward him.

"Come closer," he taunted, "and cooperate. Don't you know it will be easier for both of us . . . if you do?"

Fear, and the implication of his insinuating words, made me nauseous. I fought to free myself as grasping hands tugged at my school uniform, popping the buttons one by one. Panic and revulsion swept over me as he ripped it from my shoulders.

"Dozo! Dozo!" (Please! Please!) I begged, trying frantically to cover my exposed bosom. "Go away! Leave me alone!" Encouraged by his buddies' crude remarks and raucous laughter the officer in charge ignored my pleas. . . .

Sometime later one of the amused spectators led me back to solitary confinement. Heartsick and still trembling from the humiliation and memory of that dreadful experience, I stumbled along behind him—my body bruised and bleeding!

In the past I had doubted similar stories told by prisoners who had suffered physical abuse—brutal beatings, hot-pepper water poured in the nostrils, sexual harassment, and starvation diets. Why would anyone resort to the use of a branding iron or the so-called *water-hose treatment* to coerce or inflict pain on another human being? It seemed incongruous, and somehow I couldn't bring myself to believe these sordid tales of torture—until I had experienced them myself!

For me the interrogation room became a chamber of horrors, a nightmare of nakedness and abuse. During such a session the tip of one breast was excised because I refused to sign a confession. Without medical care the pain was excruciating. For agonizing hours I applied pressure with my fingertips to stop the flow of blood. Another day I received severe burns on both my back and bosom, wounds that were painful and slow to heal.

I came to dread the sound of clicking boots in the corridor, and each time a jailor's key turned in the lock of my cell I froze with fear. Were they going to question me again? Would my fate eventually be the same as that of Yoo Kwan Soon who had been executed during the 1919 uprising in Korea—by electrical shocks in the womb?

Political prisoners were segregated according to the severity of crimes committed. Since I was charged with treason and a high security risk, they kept me in solitary confinement away from the other inmates. Even then I had no privacy, for it was impossible to escape the guards' watchful eyes.

In my youth I had more or less become accustomed to hunger, but here inmates were kept on a starvation diet. Those who cooperated by signing a confession were given a daily dipper of water and a scoop of soybeans. Others received nothing. Sometimes my rations were withheld for days. When they did come the dry beans were difficult to digest and hard to keep down. In time my stomach shrank, and I became weak from malnutrition.

Without a doubt those months spent at the Osaka prison were the most miserable of my life. Specific details are still too painful to recall, too sadistic to record on paper. I have deliberately tried to erase them from memory, even though the telltale scars on my body will always be silent reminders of all that happened.

During those dreary days and long nights of incarceration God became my "refuge and strength, an ever present help in trouble" as never before. Continually I turned to Him for comfort and companionship. He never let me down. Furthermore, in the years since, God has taught me to forgive and forget. Although the physical scars linger, the psychological wounds have healed completely. After all, didn't the Lord Himself say, "Vengeance is mine"?

Eventually authorities transferred me by truck, along with a number of other inmates, to a prison on the outskirts of Osaka. In all of those months I had not been outside prison walls and had no idea what was happening. Now I gathered from listening to the other prisoners' conversations that Japan had made further conquests in eastern Asia. Also, after recouping their losses, the Americans were striking back. *Had Sinbo been called into combat?*

As our vehicle bumped over the ruts and ridges of country roads, I could hear other trucks pass by. No doubt they were loaded with soldiers and supplies. It seemed good to be with other people again, to fill my lungs with clean crisp air and to feel sunshine on my face. Unfortunately the brief fling soon ended.

At the new location jailors put me in another cold, concrete cell, and for several days I received nothing to eat. Finally one of the prison supervisors came to see me. "Everyone here has a work assignment," he said. "Can you sew?" I assured him that I could, and he told the guard to bring me food, as well as a box filled with soldiers' socks and clothing that needed mending. The assignment was a challenge and kept my hands busy. I was grateful for the diversion but sometimes wondered if they expected me to mend for the entire Japanese army. The task seemed endless!

Days dragged by in a meaningless procession. There was plenty of time for introspection, time to reflect on the vulnerability of life on earth, time to be thankful for life hereafter. Knowing that everything works for the good of those who love God, for those who have been called according to his purpose, I could find no room in my heart for malevolent feelings toward the Japanese people as a whole. Many had been very kind to me. No doubt they and other private citizens would be shocked to learn what had been going on behind prison walls. I prayed that God would help me be a testimony to the jailors, to be faithful to the end—as was the apostle Paul.

Regardless of how dire the circumstances and how despondent I became, there was always something for which

to be grateful. I tried to concentrate on each one. Now, at the
new location, I was not subjected to further interrogations; the
ruthless, terrorist tactics were not repeated. How grateful I
was!

Since first beginning my work assignment I had also
received daily rations—dry soybeans and a dipper of water.
My hunger was never satisfied, though, and sometimes I
dreamed about sitting down to a banquet table filled with
delicious Korean foods. At that point I would have settled for
a dish of *kimchi* and rice!

Actually, however, my worst misery was caused by
extremely cold weather and a lack of warm clothes. I still had
no bedding and the concrete cell stayed damp most of the
time. Many nights when arctic winds penetrated the building
my fingers and feet felt frozen. Even though I rubbed them
warm, frostbite eventually caused the loss of several toenails.

One morning I wakened earlier than usual. An old burn on
my abdomen had become infected, and there was no medicine
with which to treat it. My entire body felt aflame, and no
matter what position I took the pain persisted. Bedbugs also
added to my misery. At that point a warm tub bath and clean
clothes would have seemed like heaven.

As I lay there wishing for a tube of ointment and some
gauze bandages, the faint words of an old hymn drifted
through a small window overhead. I strained to hear them.
The voice sounded hauntingly familiar.

> Jesus, keep me near the cross,
> There a precious fountain
> Free to all—a healing stream,
> Flows from Calvary's mountain

Had God, knowing how much I was hurting, sent a message
to bolster my faith and give me new courage? The old words,
sung verse by verse, were like a soothing balm to my soul; and

as I lay listening it suddenly occurred to me that the rich baritone voice coming from a hilltop above the prison complex was more than vaguely familiar. I had heard that resonant voice before, many times, and would recognize it anywhere. Or had I? Was my mind merely wandering?

I listened again. The words were barely perceptible above the pounding of my heart, but now I knew for certain. It *was* Sinbo! Dear, faithful Sinbo! How had he found me? Was he trying to communicate, trying to tell me that he was standing by . . . and still cared?

Tears of joy bathed my face.

CHAPTER 18

Marriage
Proposal

"Persecuted, but not abandoned; struck down, but not destroyed" (2 Cor. 4:9). At times during those months of isolation I felt deserted by my friends, but never by God. As the dreary days dragged on my faith grew stronger. I felt the nearness of my Lord as never before!

Spring finally arrived, bringing with it warmer weather. The thrill of cherry-blossom time was to be nothing more than a pleasant memory for me that year. But I thanked God for rising temperatures and prayed for an early release, fearing that I could not survive another winter in prison without warm clothes and bedding.

While living conditions at the new location were more favorable, prison life was still dreadfully monotonous. It was difficult to keep track of time without a calendar or watch, but the warmth from a tiny patch of sunlight that shone through an overhead window gave me a clue as to whether it was day or night.

My only visitors, aside from jailors who brought daily rations and boxes of socks to mend, were insects which also enjoyed the warmer weather. Cockroaches crawled out of hibernation. Bedbugs and fleas also flourished in the filth. Soon inflamed welts covered my face and body. How they itched! I spent almost as much time scratching as darning!

In the past I had taken my Braille Bible for granted, knowing that the bulky volumes were always near at hand. Now I could only rely on memory, recalling the portions of Scripture my Sunday school teachers had encouraged me to memorize as a child. Repeating those verses now, as well as those learned at Bible school, gave me a great deal of encouragement and comfort.

Without proper ventilation the summer months seemed unusually hot and humid. The air inside my small cell was stifling, even at night, especially during the monsoon season. Rain pelted the cracked tiles for hours at a time, and I listened to the steady plunk . . . plunk . . . plunk of raindrops that dripped onto the floor in ever-widening puddles. Moisture trickled down the walls in tiny rivulets, adding to the damp, musty stench.

I was beginning to think the ordeal would never end when one day a guard unexpectedly came to my cell. Without an explanation he announced, "You have visitors. Come with me."

Company? Who could it be? I followed him to the warden's office, not knowing what to expect.

"Chung Syn, my dear. How are you?"

"Dr. Okawa!" I reached out to shake his hand. "This is a wonderful surprise. Why are you here?"

"We have come to take you home."

"When?" I asked in disbelief.

"Now! This very minute!" he exclaimed. "The new semester is already getting under way. You will only have a few days to rest before classes begin."

Mixed emotions swept over me. Happiness! Relief!

Gratitude! Humiliation! The latter almost overshadowed the joy of being released. My clothes were dirty and ragged. There had been no opportunity to launder them. And in all those months I'd had neither a bath nor a shampoo. My daily ration of water was small, barely enough to quench thirst, and even during the rainy season there had been nothing in which to catch the precious drips.

"We?" I asked timidly. "Who . . . who came with you?"

"Dr. Hujida," he answered. "She is now a full-fledged physician and wants to look after you herself. She's waiting in the taxi outside." I smiled with relief, grateful that Sinbo hadn't come too. He was the last person I wanted to see me looking like a beggar!

"There's nothing to hold us here, Chung Syn. Your papers are all in order."

"You mean I've been cleared of espionage . . . and all the other false charges?"

"Not exactly. You see, charges were never filed."

It took a few seconds for the full impact of his words to register. "Do you mean this was . . . for nothing?"

"I guess you could say that, but believe me we did everything possible. It took time to cut all the red tape and convince them of your innocence."

My first reaction was one of indignation. Then stubbornness took over, and I refused to leave. "The least they can do is apologize," I protested. "I'll stay here until they do."

Dr. Okawa took my arm and steered me toward the door. "Don't tempt fate, my dear. Let's leave while we can. Nothing will be accomplished by creating a scene."

Bitterness overwhelmed me. It would take time, maturity, and the grace of God working in my heart to help me forget those torturous months in prison and to forgive those who had caused my suffering.

Outside Dr. Hujida, who had been a senior student when I left, hugged me affectionately. "Oh Chung Syn, how good it is to see you." She held me at arm's length. "You look a bit thin."

"And dirty," I laughed. "How are things at school?"

"Fine."

"And Sinbo? Have you seen him?"

"Oh yes. Sinbo will come by your apartment this evening. He thought you might need time . . . before having company. He has really missed you. We all have."

"That's good to hear. Sometimes I thought the whole world had forgotten me. It was dreadful."

"I know, but the nightmare is over. Now you must try to forget. Where would you like to go first?"

"Straight to the public baths."

"No sooner said than done. I went by your room and picked up some clean clothes." I must have really looked a sight—skinny, scaly, and covered with flea bites. But she made no comment about my condition until starting to soap my back.

"Where did you get these scars?" she asked. "They look like burns. And what happened to your breast? The . . . the nipple is missing!"

When I told her of my ordeal, she wept. But nothing, *nothing* could dampen my spirits. I was intoxicated with the exhilaration of freedom. I was free again! Free to breathe fresh air, free to bathe, free to come and go as I pleased. How wonderful it seemed!

Never before and never since has a bath been so welcome or felt so good. I soaked in that hot sudsy water until my skin puckered like a prune.

Later my two friends took me home. Everything was just as I had left it. My books were still on the table, my clothes still hung in the closet. Slowly I walked around the small room, touching every familiar object with my fingers. Tears of gratitude welled inside when I discovered that my landlady had brought in a pot of soup for my supper. How delicious it tasted. Believe me, I savored every morsel, right down to the last noodle.

That same evening Sinbo and his mother came. She held me in her arms and wept, repeating over and over again how glad she was to see me.

When we were alone for a few moments Sinbo simply said, "I thought this day would never come. I've missed you so very, very much." My heart nearly burst. Hearing his dear voice again and feeling the tenderness of his touch filled me with indescribable joy—joy that made all the pain fade into oblivion.

We brewed a pot of tea and talked . . . and talked, it seemed for hours, about all that had happened since we parted. I learned that Sinbo had dropped out of school. "I wanted us to finish together," he explained, "so I could help you." He took both of my hands in his. "Not once did I give up hope, Chung Syn. I knew that sooner or later God would answer my prayers . . . and bring you back."

"He answered both of our prayers. You'll never know how much it encouraged me to hear you singing one of my favorite hymns that day. I couldn't believe it!"

He laughed, that soft endearing chuckle that I remembered so well. "Did you recognize my voice right away?"

"Oh yes, but I was almost afraid to believe my ears. For a minute I thought my mind was playing tricks. But tell me, were you surprised to come back from field assignment and find that the police had taken me away? How have you stayed out of the army? I thought you might be drafted by now. Did Dr. Okawa tell you that my scholarship is still available?"

Sinbo laughed again. "Slow down. One question at a time. Yes, I knew about your scholarship. Dr. Okawa has been a wonderful friend, in every way. He kept in close contact with the police and finally learned where they had taken you. He's worked for months trying to get you released."

"I'm ashamed of myself."

"Why?" he asked.

"Because . . . I thought everyone had forgotten me."

"Surely you knew better than that. You were in my thoughts and prayers constantly. I feel dreadful about things that have happened." His voice broke. "I hope to make it all up to you someday . . . after we've finished school." My heart skipped a beat, but I didn't dare speculate about his reference to the future. Time would take care of that. For now it was enough just to be together again.

"What have you been doing all these months?"

"Working at the hospital as an orderly and medical technician. Unfortunately the war isn't over yet, and our casualties have been heavy."

Finally Sinbo's mother interrupted our conversation. "Son, Chung Syn is exhausted. You two can talk to your hearts' content . . . later."

The three of us prayed together before they left. Then, for the first time in months, I slipped between clean sheets. How can I describe what a pleasant sensation it was to luxuriate beneath a clean, cozy comforter in familiar surroundings? Yet, weary as I was, sleep came slowly. So much had happened so fast; it took time to unwind.

Dr. Okawa insisted on admitting me to the hospital for a check up. "I want to keep an eye on you for a few days. After all, we can't afford to lose one of our top doctoral candidates."

My friend seemed worried about a recurrence of tuberculosis. Subconsciously I shared his concern. But when the test results were in we were both relieved. "There is nothing wrong with you," he assured, "that rest and nourishing food won't cure completely. We'll keep you here for several days . . . and pamper you a bit." The nurses, all Japanese, did just that. They seemed determined to make up for the neglect and abuse I had suffered in prison.

I thrived on the excellent care, dozing during the day and sleeping through the nights. My appetite was insatiable, and I ate all the in-between snacks set before me, sending my mealtime trays back to the kitchen empty. Food had never tasted better!

Two weeks after my release from prison Sinbo and I were back in medical school again—side by side. Our former classmates, knowing that he had deliberately waited for my return, heckled and teased him about flunking last year's courses, but Sinbo didn't mind. He seemed satisfied just to be my faithful shadow once more.

My junior year was busy, sometimes hectic. In addition to attending classes and clinical demonstrations I still gave treatments at the hospital, occasionally arriving home late at night. One evening I left the campus during a downpour, confident that I could walk to the trolley stop without any problem. Rain, however, makes it difficult for a blind person to find his or her way. With water blowing in my face I soon lost my non-visual perception and inadvertently wandered into a narrow alley. Intuition told me that I had made a wrong turn when my foot struck something—a soft, unyielding object. Thrown off balance I stumbled and almost fell.

Instantly hands clutched at my skirt. "Who kicked me?" a stranger snarled. "Why don'cha watch wher' yu're goin?" His words were slurred and run together.

I backed away. "Forgive me, sir. I am blind . . . and didn't see you lying there." Guided by the sounds of traffic I turned and retraced my steps. Apparently the drunk staggered to his feet and followed me, for I heard shuffling footsteps close behind as I ran back to the street, stumbling and screaming for help. Attracted by the commotion a policeman came to my rescue, later volunteering to escort me as far as the trolley. I accepted his offer with gratitude and after that tried not to travel in the rain by myself.

It is amazing how quickly time passes when one is busy doing something enjoyable and challenging. The next two years whizzed by, and before I realized it graduation was upon me. By then conditions in Japan were stark, food supplies short, and nerves jangled. World War II still raged, with the confrontations in eastern Asia coming disturbingly close to home. During recent months the Japanese army had suffered severe losses, and it was rumored that American aircraft carriers with long-range bombers aboard had been sighted too close for comfort.

Japan needed additional doctors in a hurry. So students at Misima were given a crash course in treating casualties, and the faculty condensed our curriculum, covering the same material in a shorter period of time. They also decided, in order to make interns available for military service, to hold our graduation early.

Because of this national emergency the deadline to turn in our doctoral theses was mid-January. I chose the subject of "Recurrent Fever" for my paper and had completed most of the research prior to the surprise announcement. When my thesis was finally finished, Sinbo insisted on transcribing the Braille notes and typing them in finished form.

"But you have your own to do," I protested, "besides cramming for finals."

"Don't worry about it. 'Where there's a will, there's a way.' I'll pick up your notes this afternoon and get started over the weekend. Once they're transcribed the typing won't take long."

When I returned to my room after a busy day of clinical demonstrations, I found several sheets of paper still on the table. Quickly my fingers skimmed over the raised dots to

determine whether Sinbo had missed some of my notes.
Instead I found that he had left me a Brailled letter:

Dearest Chung Syn,

   I hope you will read this letter prayerfully and that you will
not make up your mind until we can talk it over.
   Surely in the past five years you have come to realize how
much I care for you, so this proposal should come as no
surprise. Our time here at Misima is almost over, and soon we
must make some important decisions about the future.
   We both know that marriage is a sacred commitment for
Christians, . . . a union of body, mind, and soul. I feel that God
has brought us together for this very reason, and that we could
serve Him as husband and wife far more effectively than either
of us can alone.

My heart soared with happiness as I read and reread the
last line. "Please, Chung Syn, will you honor me by becoming
my bride?"
Never had I been so overjoyed or so filled with emotion!
The most wonderful man in the world had asked me to marry
him, and my first impulse was to shout, "Yes! Yes, of course!"
How could I refuse? Sinbo loved me! And I loved him!
Suddenly all the pieces of the puzzle were falling into place.
Before, I hadn't dare admit, even to myself, how much I cared
for this thoughtful, unselfish man of God. Now I realized
beyond a shadow of a doubt that Sinbo was to be the *one* and
only love of my life!
For some the realization of love comes swiftly. Like striking
a match, darkness turns instantly to light. For Sinbo and me it
had been slower and more subtle, a caring, sharing
relationship that with time had turned into a rich and
rewarding romance.
As I lay awake that night thinking of the future and trying
to imagine the thrill of being Sinbo's wife, a small voice within

seemed to whisper, "Chung Syn, have you forgotten the
promise you once made to serve the Lord in Korea?" Instantly
my castles started to crumble. Yes, for a few hours I had
forgotten! Now the past came back with painful clarity.

For the rest of that night I tossed, torn between a personal
desire to stay in Japan with the man I loved and the
commitment I had made many years before to serve God in
Korea . . . alone. My heart kept urging, *Marry Sinbo, Chung
Syn. You have every right to happiness!* But my mind argued,
*Remember your vow! You are needed back home—in the place of your
birth. How could you ever be happy knowing that you had broken your
promise?*

Sinbo spent the entire weekend working on our term papers.
So I didn't see him again until Monday morning. The first
thing he asked when we met on campus was, "Did you find
my note?"

I nodded. "You have greatly honored me, Sinbo."

Impulsively he reached for my hand. "Then . . . your
answer is yes?"

"Wait a minute . . . please," I whispered. "Your proposal
came as such a surprise. I need more time . . . time to think it
over and ask God for guidance. Let's talk about it later . . .
after graduation."

Sinbo squeezed my fingers before releasing them. "I will
wait, my love, for as long as you say. In the meantime I shall
be praying too . . . that someday we can serve the Lord
together."

CHAPTER 19

Sayonara

Graduation followed close on the heels of final exams. Each detail of that day still stands out in memory, for it marked one of the most thrilling and significant events of my life.

Sinbo and I marched down the aisle together, side-by-side, while his mother proudly watched from a front-row seat. Before passing out diplomas Dr. Okawa called the two of us to the microphone and pinned a red rose on my graduation gown as a symbol of victory and distinction.

"It gives me great pleasure," he told the audience, "to present a special award of merit to this young lady who graduates today with honors. As many of you know, Miss Yang has the unique distinction of being the first, and only, blind student to earn a medical degree from the Misima School of Medicine."

Later he lauded Sinbo for his outstanding academic achievements and commended him for the ingenious, unselfish manner in which he had assisted me. We both returned to our seats, accompanied by enthusiastic applause. Certainly Sinbo deserved the plaudits he received, for without his help I would not have been among the grateful graduates.

I was scheduled to leave Osaka two days after the ceremony to start my internship at a hospital in Tokyo. In addition to packing I had a long list of special people—like Dr. Okawa, Dean Kanezawa, and Sinbo's mother—to thank and bid farewell.

It is always difficult to say *sayonara* to those we love. For weeks I had been dreading to tell Sinbo my decision, but the time had come to give him my answer. It wasn't fair to make him wait any longer. How should I say it? Would he understand?

Emotionally I was a woman with natural drives and desires. I longed to be Sinbo's wife . . . to make him happy . . . to share his home and mother his children. Yet logic told me this could never be. I had already committed myself, and all of the rationalizations in the world could not alter that.

I finally invited Sinbo to drop by my apartment for a cup of tea. He arrived in a philosophical mood. "Isn't it hard to realize that our school days are over, Chung Syn? I mean . . . Dr. Yang," he corrected. "Seems such a short while ago that I first saw you sitting there in anatomy class, puzzling over an assignment. You looked so little . . . and so lost."

"And do you remember the frog episode?" I laughed.

"You were so frustrated and furious. I couldn't understand —threatening to quit school over a frog."

"If you hadn't been so persistent that morning, my medical career might have ended before it started. Your forcefulness is one of the things I admire about you most—and that's quite a concession coming from someone who doesn't like to be told what to do."

"Confession is good for the soul, doctor. Tell me more," Sinbo coaxed. "Besides, I like what you're saying."

"Stop teasing. I'm serious. You can't know how much I appreciate all you have done."

"Enough to marry me?" he asked soberly.

I couldn't dodge the issue any longer. The time had come to give him an honest answer. "Your proposal of marriage has honored me, Sinbo. But. . . ."

"But?" he asked, holding my hand to his cheek. "But what? You aren't in love with me?"

"No, I didn't say that. You mean a great deal to me, but I am not free to marry."

"Are you promised to someone in Korea?" he asked, his voice strangely subdued.

"Yes. In a way I am, Sinbo. You see . . . several years ago, even before we met, I made a sacred promise to serve God for the rest of my life if He would help me get a good education. I was without money at the time, in debt, and struggling to pay my tuition. God heard my prayers and provided a job. Since then He has met every need. I can't forget that vow."

"But you don't have to. You know I want to serve God too. We have a great deal in common. That is what has made our relationship so special. We can work together, as medical missionaries," he enthused. "There are Japanese villages without a hospital or church. Maybe we could open a clinic . . . and later build a church."

I couldn't let him go on. "Please, Sinbo, try to understand. Your heart is *here*, but I am needed in Korea. There are so many spiritually blind people in my country who will never see the light—unless someone tells them about Jesus. Besides . . . I took a vow never to marry."

"But you were too young then to understand the consequences," he insisted. "Surely you don't think God will hold you to an unrealistic promise, one you made while still a child?"

"Sinbo, do you remember what it says in Psalm 15 about keeping a solemn promise once it is made—even though it hurts? For weeks I tried to get those words out of my mind, but they keep haunting me."

Sinbo set his cup on the *chow* table before us and took both of my hands in his. "When we first met I was drawn to you because of your total commitment to Christ, and I wanted to be of help."

"You were sorry for me. Right?"

"Maybe, in the beginning. But before long I realized what a wonderful person you are, and slowly but surely I found myself falling in love. Besides," he added with a chuckle, "you're cute."

"And you, my friend, are impossible! Thoughtful, generous, wonderful . . . and impossible!"

"You forgot to add persistent. Chung Syn, you still haven't answered my question. Do you care for me?"

I nodded. "Very much, my dear. There is nothing in this world I would rather be . . . than your wife." He intertwined his fingers with mine, and I hurried on. "But how can I turn my back on the Lord? Could either of us be happy, really happy, knowing that I had broken a sacred pledge?"

Suddenly Sinbo released my hand and walked to the window. He stood for a few seconds in silence while searching for a solution. "I understand how you feel," he finally said. "But let's not make a hasty decision. We both need time to think. I'll come to Tokyo after finishing my internship, sooner if possible. We can talk it over again. Until then I'll stay in touch by mail."

Sinbo's mother gave a small farewell party for me the night before I left, and the next morning Sinbo took me to the train station. Parting was painful for both of us. He still hoped we could make a future together, but I knew this would never be and for that reason longed to look on his face—just once. Instead I had only the sound of Sinbo's voice and his parting words to remember.

He stood on the platform and held my hand through an open window. "*Sayonara,* Chung Syn," he whispered. "Be

patient . . . and may God go with you." As the train started to
roll he called, "Don't forget me and . . . write."

"I will, Sinbo. Take care of yourself." Long after my train
had pulled out of the station and gained momentum I still
stood by the window and waved.

The chief of staff at the Shiowa Hospital, where I was to
intern, assigned me to internal medicine. Three nurse
assistants were, in a sense, to be my eyes. He gave me several
days to become oriented to hospital procedures and
familiarize myself with the surroundings before starting work
on the ward. The sighted staff, as well as the patients,
responded to my blindness with varied reactions. Some were
skeptical about my qualifications, other considered me a sort
of wonder-woman. In either case I knew it would be up to me
to prove myself.

We worked long shifts and were on call around the clock. I
enjoyed my new responsibilities and the challenges involved
but missed talking things over with Sinbo. I looked forward to
his letters, each one filled with endearing words of
encouragement.

In order to expose us to as many phases of the medical
profession as possible, interns were rotated from one
department to another. I enjoyed each new assignment, since
long hours and hard work kept me from being lonely. Nights I
fell asleep just as soon as my head touched my pillow.

One morning a hemorrhaging woman was admitted to my
ward. A preliminary examination revealed that she suffered
from acute endometriosis. I recommended surgery, and a
consulting physician concurred with my diagnosis.

Because he was short-staffed, the resident surgeon asked me
to assist him. Afterward he seemed pleased and surprised by
my competence.

"You amaze me," he confided. "I have never seen anyone
with such sensitive fingers." After that he often invited

me to come in as a consultant or assistant, and in time I did simple operations under his guidance. Eventually, with the help of sighted staff members, I performed a successful hysterectomy. Such experiences were challenging, and earning the respect of my colleagues gave me a great deal of satisfaction.

Since many young doctors had been called into military service, those of us who weren't found ourselves doing double duty. By the conclusion of my internship I was totally exhausted from overwork.

Sinbo, aware of my penchant for overdoing, wrote and urged me to take a vacation. "You need a change of pace. Why not go home and visit your family for a few weeks?" he asked. "I am eager to see you and will come to Tokyo just as soon as you return."

American bombers were making nightly raids on Japanese cities. Surrender seemed imminent, and I knew the time had come for me to return home. After turning in my resignation at the hospital, I packed and Brailled a farewell note to the man I loved.

Dearest Sinbo,

You are right. I do need a vacation and have decided to follow your advice. I am returning to Korea permanently. Please try to understand. My decision was made after much thought and prayer.

I love you, Sinbo, and it will not be easy for me to leave Japan. A part of my heart will always be here with you. So will my thoughts.

Thank you for everything—your encouragement, faithfulness, and marriage proposal. I shall cherish memories of you and the good times we've shared for the rest of my life.

Just as you have loved me, Sinbo, you will learn to love again. I am sure God has someone special for you. I wish with all my heart it could be me.

Under the circumstances it will be best if we don't keep in touch. For that reason I am not enclosing my future address. *Sayonara,* Sinbo, and may God watch over you always.

With all my love and gratitude,
Chung Syn

My heart was heavy as I posted that last letter to Sinbo, the man who had become so dear to me. Life without him would not be the same!

Enroute to Shimonoseki the train passed through Osaka, and when a gruff-voiced conductor announced the stop in advance, I found myself embroiled in an emotional tug of war. I longed to hear Sinbo's voice, to feel his arms around me, and to have his lips touch mine, if only for a moment. Yet I knew if we met again neither of us would have the strength to part.

It was all I could do to stay seated as other passengers streamed down the aisle. I wanted to follow them, to find Sinbo and stay by his side. Instead I sat in silence, tears trickling down my cheeks, as the train wheels stopped . . . then slowly gathered momentum.

Several hours later I stood at the dock waiting to purchase a ticket for Korea. As familiar sounds came to my ears, memories of another day came to my mind. It was here at Shimonoseki that I, an expectant young woman eagerly looking forward to a musical career, had first set foot on Japanese soil. Then I had wondered what kind of reception a blind, Korean student would receive. Now I was headed home, wiser and more mature, but still wondering what the future held in store. Would my own people accept a sightless doctor? Would they reject me? Only time would tell.

Because of the war civilian travelers were low on the priority list. I was told there would be a one-week wait. During the long layover I became acquainted with a young Japanese woman and her small child. They were traveling to

Korea, where the baby's father was now stationed. I sensed the young woman was fearful of traveling alone.

On departure day we learned that two ships would be sailing—one that morning, the other that night. My boarding pass was for the early crossing; Mrs. Maesaba's was for the latter.

"Please trade with me," she begged. "It's hard to travel at night with a baby. Besides, I am deathly afraid of water!"

I felt sorry for the young mother, but my luggage had already gone aboard. It was too late to make a switch.

As I walked away she grabbed my jacket. "Have mercy on me, doctor. You can claim your luggage again at the dock in Pusan. Please?"

I too was weary of waiting and didn't look forward to another idle day, but because the young mother seemed so desperate I agreed to exchange boarding passes. Mrs. Maesaba, sounding greatly relieved, thanked me several times before walking up the gangplank. The child slept, strapped on her back.

That evening just before dusk the second ship shoved off, and I was aboard. We were immediately issued life jackets and warned to stay inside with the portholes closed. "We are traveling under black-out restrictions, but there is nothing to worry about. Weather conditions are favorable, and we should reach Pusan by mid-morning," the first mate told us.

Three hours later a series of vibrating jolts brought the ship to a sudden stop. Crew members shouted from the deck! Passengers inside became panicky, some screaming, others crying—all fearing enemy action. I stayed in my seat and prayed as fellow travelers milled about, most excitedly speculating on what had happened. One woman thought we had collided with another ship. Someone else shouted that we had been torpedoed by a submarine.

Finally the captain's reassuring voice came over the

loudspeaker. "We have stopped to make rescues," he explained. "Our sister ship was sunk here this morning, and we have sighted several lifeboats." His voice dropped. "Most appear to be empty."

My heart nearly stopped! Mrs. Maesaba and her baby were aboard that ship! If she hadn't begged me to trade tickets I would have been there instead! *Why, Lord?* I questioned, my thoughts in a quandry. *Why did you spare my life? What is it that you have for me to do?*

Our ship circled the oil-blackened waters until early morning looking for survivors and picking up bodies of men, women, and children, some already showing signs of bloat. Mrs. Maesaba and her little one were never found. A few brave passengers watched rescue operations from the deck, but most of us stayed inside. When they described the tragic scene I told them that, in this case, blindness was a blessing.

Occasionally a plane zoomed overhead. Each time I wondered whether it was a friend or foe and didn't breathe easily again until the sound of its engines faded into the distance. We all wore life jackets as a precautionary measure and received instructions from the crew on how to board the lifeboats. In the back of my mind was the apprehension that somewhere beneath the surface an enemy submarine might still be lurking, waiting to make us its next target. Yet, through it all, I felt amazingly calm, knowing that God was in control and that my life was in His hands.

Our captain, in order to avoid the same misfortune that had befallen his sister ship, charted a new course, crossing the Sea of Japan by a zigzag route. Eventually the sturdy little ship steamed into Yosu harbor—but not before the trip, which normally took a day or less, had stretched into three.

I followed the other passengers ashore as they hastily disembarked. No one was more grateful than I to feel Korean soil beneath my feet, to walk again in the land of my birth.

CHAPTER 20

Flight to Freedom

It was wonderful to be home! After our close call at sea I thanked God for safety. Nothing else mattered. All of my possessions, everything I had accumulated during my stay in Japan, except for a handbag and the clothes on my back, had gone down with the torpedoed ship. But following our recent brush with death these material things seemed relatively unimportant.

At Yosu I heard good news. The Japanese empire was on the verge of collapse, and many high ranking government officials had already returned to Japan. Believing it would now be safe for me in Pyongyang, I purchased a ticket and left immediately. Much to my surprise I found that the scene had changed considerably in the past five or six years. The Hills were no longer living there; most of my former classmates had scattered.

After spending some time as a patient at Kitok Hospital I accepted a position as instructor at their Christian School of Nursing. The young women were receptive, and even doctors attended my lectures. They seemed eager to learn Japan's

more modern and innovative medical techniques. I spent my
days off working with blind children at Chung-Jin. I loved the
youngsters, understood their problems, and hoped to someday
found an orphanage where needy children could receive a
good education free of charge.

Keeping busy kept me from being lonely, but it wasn't
possible to forget the past overnight. My mind often wandered
to Sinbo, reliving the good times we had together and
wondering where he was. I knew if Sinbo were here he would
encourage me to pursue my dreams.

My first goal was to open a clinic at Sariwon with the
assistance of my sister Yu-nok, now a nurse. I applied for a
license; passed an examination given by the Korean medical
board, and received a permit to open a small medical facility.

Because war demands took priority, obtaining medical
supplies was a chore. Even bandages and simple medicines
such as aspirin were in short supply, but finally I acquired the
necessary equipment and rented a small building. Then, after
hiring another nurse, I hung out my shingle—the first blind
woman doctor to practice medicine in that vicinity. I called
the place Cha-He Clinic (Grace and Mercy Clinic).

The sick and the curious came, one by one. The first day we
had five patients, the next ten, and before long more ailing
people than we could handle came through the clinic doors
during a single day. Sometimes I worked until late at night.
No one was turned away for lack of funds. We treated both the
affluent and the poor. Those who had no money were
encouraged to pay at a later date. This kept the needy from
feeling like charity cases.

I had some narrow escapes. Once a drunken man
brandishing a samurai sword accosted me in my office late at
night. On another occasion I was robbed in a dark alley by the
rickshaw driver who came to pick me up after I had delivered
a baby. I also had a couple tenacious suitors, both of whom

proposed marriage and were promptly rejected. My heart was still in Japan!

We all breathed a sigh of relief when Emperor Hirohito, on August 15, 1945, surrendered unconditionally to the Allied forces! After forty years of harsh treatment and harassment, Japanese troops withdrew. But our trials were not yet over! As a result of the Potsdam Declaration, Korea was divided at the thirty-eighth parallel. Friendly Americans took over protection of the south, hostile Russians occupied the north. Pyongyang, once the missionary center of Korea, was turned into a communist capital, and Koreans again lived in fear.

Russian soldiers who swooped down from the north plundered and intimidated as they went. Fearful of their tactics I closed the clinic and stored most of my equipment in an office building abandoned by a Japanese dentist. The Teis, a wealthy and influential family whose lame son I had cured with acupuncture treatments, invited me to live in their suburban Sariwon home. It was with them that I later managed to escape from North Korea.

On April 14, 1946, a date long to be remembered, we boarded a train for Haeju, taking with us only the bare essentials. Later we loaded our bundles into an ox cart and moved cautiously past Sun-on Temple. Near a small village we were stopped by an old farmer who offered to guide us.

Father Tei didn't trust the fellow. "He's furtive and shifty-eyed," he explained. "I suspect he's trying to trick us."

"But we need help," I reminded him. "We'll never make it to freedom alone."

Father Tei reluctantly agreed. "You're right. Every road is guarded by communist troops."

After we promised the stranger a generous fee for his services, he took us to an isolated farmhouse. There we found several other nervous fugitives, all waiting for nightfall. Toward evening the farmer's wife served us a simple meal.

Then, under cover of darkness, we started our trek southward, hoping to make it through communist territory before dawn.

The old man led us over dusty, untraveled trails. We quietly crept through woods and open fields, climbed hills, and crawled over fences before coming to the river. The last mile and a half was treacherous. We waded through icy, thigh-high water; several times I slipped and nearly fell.

Finally, as we crawled up the steep bank on the other side—tired, covered with mud, and shivering from the cold—our guide announced, "You are in South Korea. Good luck!" Without another word he collected his fee and disappeared into the morning shadows.

We had made it! But what price freedom? The Teis had left behind a fortune. I had closed my clinic and had said farewell to all of my family. (Although three of us—Yu-nok, Teuk-Choon, and I—were later united in the south, our parents remained under communist control.)

A sudden influx of refugees caused a housing shortage in Seoul. After sharing an upstairs flat with two squabbling, unscrupulous families, I finally rented a drafty, dilapidated building on the edge of town. The roof leaked, and the thin walls had chink holes, but my maid and I were both grateful for privacy. Mornings I attended Hankuk Theological Seminary; afternoons I saw patients in my makeshift office.

I had just returned from preaching at a nearby church one Sunday afternoon when the sound of someone clearing his throat drifted through the open door. This was the traditional way for Korean guests to announce their arrival. My brother, who lived with me at the time, answered the summons and found a friend of the Hills standing outside. He said the Hills were living in Ansong. After that I visited them often; it was great to be together again. Our long conversations eventually snipped away the years of separation.

Then, on June 25, 1950, the North Koreans swooped across

the thirty-eighth parallel. In General MacArthur's words, "The *In Min Gun* struck like a cobra." Within seventy-two hours communist troops stormed Seoul. Civilians fled on foot. With mortar shells and bombs dropping around us we hid among the ruins—in fields, cellars, and burned-out buildings. One time I even curled up in the brick oven of a farmhouse while soldiers searched the premises.

Through it all my maid, Soon-ok, was a faithful friend. She never left me, though at times we had little to eat. When there was rice in the pantry we shared it with others, and after it disappeared God graciously supplied more. Church congregations were generous, and somehow we managed to get by.

We were elated to hear that American GIs had landed at Inchon, happier still when we heard American tanks rumble through the countryside. Help was on the way!

When civilians were able to return to Seoul, Soon-ok and I found that our house had been hit. Nothing remained but a heap of rubble. The seminary was also destroyed, but later rebuilt; and I received my bachelor of divinity degree in July, 1951.

American General Sherman once said, "War is hell." He was right! During the holocaust a million civilians lost their lives. Millions more were left homeless. Military casualties were also heavy. Numbers of young soldiers lost their sight, so I was asked to help in an effort to rehabilitate and teach these young men to cope with blindness. I also counseled and encouraged soldiers who returned from the front, giving them promises from God's Word.

After preaching at a service in Taegu one night I asked someone from the audience to close with prayer. A young army lieutenant responded. I was deeply touched by his sincerity. Later he introduced himself.

"My name is Heung Syn," he said. "You may not remember me. It's been several years now."

"Of course I do. You accepted the Lord at one of my meetings. How is your mother?" Heung (now Dr. Henry Syn) was the son of an old acquaintance.

"Mother is fine. She sends her regards. We heard you were speaking here tonight, and I wanted to see you again before leaving."

"Leaving?" I asked.

"My regiment is being sent to the front lines." He paused. "Would you have time to write to me, Dr. Yang?"

"I will pray for you, too, Heung . . . every day."

After that, each time he returned home on furlough Henry visited me. He was a sensitive, serious young man and very burdened about conditions in Korea. We had long talks about things of the Lord, and it was a genuine thrill to watch his faith grow. In between, I wrote to him, trying to encourage and keep up his morale.

Eventually Henry was sent home on medical furlough. Army doctors attributed his weight loss, depression, and severe headaches to battle fatigue. When rest and medication failed to relieve the symptoms Henry consulted me. I located his problem, and after a short series of acupuncture treatments he was able to rejoin his company on the front lines.

On July 27, 1953, the Korean War ended! How grateful we were to our American allies who helped stop the ruthless blood bath that had lasted three years and had claimed the lives of many innocent people. Even after the cease-fire, however, pandemonium continued. Sections of Seoul had been reduced to rubble. There were now hundreds of war widows and orphans in the capital city. Some lived in makeshift lean-tos and shanties, others in the ruins of bombed-out buildings. The Red Cross and organizations from overseas did what they could. But there wasn't enough rice to go around!

For the past two years I had served, first as secretary of the Lighthouse in Pusan, and then as dean of the Blind and Deaf School at Taegu. Conditions around the country were pitiful, and it broke my heart to know that young girls were becoming women of the streets, selling favors to soldiers for money to buy food, while abandoned children and orphans were forced to steal or become beggars in order to survive. I longed to tell each one about Jesus and to give them a new lease on life. My dream of starting an orphanage for blind children had never dimmed, and at that point I was more determined than ever.

In the fall of 1953 that nebulous dream became a reality! With the assistance and support of my Presbyterian friends I rented an old house in Chonju, made a few necessary repairs, and opened the doors of our little orphanage. We begged, borrowed, and did everything but steal in order to make ends meet, operating for the most part under auspices of the Christian Children's Fund. Many generous Americans helped by *adopting an orphan.* Their ten-dollar monthly contributions supported and provided care for one child.

We started with five children—four girls and one boy. They were dirty, neglected little waifs, but I loved each one. As our enrollment grew it was difficult for me and another young woman to cope with a houseful of rambunctious children. Our students needed a man's influence—someone with a voice of authority who could provide a father image.

Shortly after I started praying for such an assistant, Henry came home on furlough. His heart went out to these little strays, and needless to say Captain Syn soon became the children's hero. After his discharge from the military Henry joined our staff full time. With the vibrance of youth, he taught the children to sing, run, laugh, play games, and think positively.

"You may be blind," he told them, "but that's no

handicap—unless you let it be! God gave you good minds! Learn to use them!" Henry made learning fun, and the children responded to him like flowers to sunshine. In a very short time I came to love this consecrated young man as my own son.

Little Kim was one of our more tenacious students. Although she sometimes needed discipline, Kim's mind was as absorbent as a thirsty sponge. Henry, recognizing the little girl's musical ability, gave her vocal lessons after school, and today Kim Wicks is serving the Lord in America, using her beautiful voice to sing for the glory of God.

After the orphanage was well established and became the Chonju Home and School for Blind Children I began exploring the possibility of visiting America the beautiful. I wanted to study at her universities and learn for myself what made this country so great and blessed by God. But each time I applied for a scholarship something came up to block the way. Helen Keller offered me an opportunity to study in Canada, but I declined.

Even after everything was arranged in the States I had to fight Korean bureaucracy and red tape all the way to the top. Those at lower levels of government still thought a blind person would present a *poor image* in a foreign country. My past history of tuberculosis was also a deterrent, and I had to prove my fluency with the English language. The more opposition I received the more determined I became to break through the barrier. Before finally receiving a passport and visa I had visited the Ministry of Foreign Affairs, the Attorney General's office and the Vice President of Korea. It had been a long battle, but victory was sweet!

When all signals were "go" Henry took me to the ship. "I'll join you, mom," he promised, "just as soon as I've saved money for my passage."

In San Francisco I enrolled as an education major at the

city's state university. Fellow students were warm and
friendly. "What shall we call you?" one asked.

"My name is Chung Syn. In Korean it means *Bright
Promise.*"

"That's too hard to remember," she retorted. "We need to
give you a new name . . . something short and snappy. I know!
We'll call you Chris!"

"Chris?" I asked.

"Yes, Chris is short for chrysanthemum. And you remind
me of a lovely oriental flower." Others soon picked up the
nickname and it remained with me for the entire time I stayed
in the States.

Henry arrived a short time later—with a few dollars and a
pocket full of dreams. After he found employment we moved
into a small apartment. Henry worked as a houseboy,
handyman, dishwasher, and even scrubbed toilets in order to
support us both while we attended San Francisco State
University for four years.

I graduated in June 1960, with a B.A. in education and two
years later received my master's degree from Pepperdine
University in Los Angeles. It was time to make a decision
about the future. Nearly seven wonderful years had already
slipped by. The generous people of America had accepted me
with open arms, and the Christian fellowship we shared was
sweet. After tasting fruit from the Garden of Eden, who wants
to leave it behind? What should I do—return home or stay in
the country where opportunities were beyond my wildest
dreams?

Not wanting to be unduly swayed by emotion I first prayed
about the decision, then sent out several job resumés. Each
application came back with essentially the same message:
"Sorry, but we have no openings for someone with your
qualifications." I had my answer. It was time to start packing!

Saying good-by to American friends wasn't easy. I would

especially miss Henry and his lovely wife, Soon. But my adopted son had plans of his own now. He hoped to someday return to Korea as a pastor. When, and if he did come, I would be waiting.

My own work in the "Land of Morning Calm" was not yet finished!

Reflections

It has been twenty years since Dr. Yang left Los Angeles and returned to Korea. Since then she has ministered to the sick and needy, giving of herself with the same unselfishness and compassion that has characterized her entire life. Modest about her own accomplishments and shy when it comes to accepting personal praise, she avoids the spotlight when possible, preferring to work quietly behind the scenes.

Dr. Yang's zeal and love for the Lord have not diminished with time. At an age when many men and women are looking forward to retirement and a life of leisure, Chung Syn is still serving God with fervor, unwavering faith, and singleness of purpose. Observers cannot be around this winsome woman for long without feeling enriched and inspired. Her enthusiasm is contagious!

When asked if she regrets leaving the luxuries and comforts of California to work in the land of her birth, Dr. Yang answers with a thoughtful smile. "I miss my friends, of course, but have no regrets. For I am convinced that this is where God wants me to be." A note of amusement creeps into her voice as she adds, "You are probably wondering how much one blind woman can accomplish, right? Very little alone," she admits. "But 'I can do *everything* through Him who gives me strength.'"

For a time Dr. Yang taught theology at the seminary in Seoul where she earned her bachelor's degree. Teaching the inerrancy of God's Word to eager young minds was gratifying, but she discovered that doctrinal differences were causing dissension among her constituents. Not wanting to become involved in such disputes, and also desiring to fill a pulpit herself, Chung Syn resigned to pursue other challenging activities—preaching, counseling, and working with men behind bars.

Dr. Yang's personal prison ministry has been lucrative in terms of salvaged lives. Her message to inmates is simple and straight to the point: "We have all sinned and come short of God's glory," she tells them. "Not one of us—no one—is righteous. Without the Lord in our lives we are lost, beyond hope. But I have good news for everyone here. God forgives sinners like you and me!

"Anyone who is in Christ is a new creature. Old things pass away; all things become new. No matter what you and I have done in the past, regardless of how severe our sins, God will forgive us . . . if we ask Him to, for anyone who calls on the Lord's name will be saved."

To prison inmates Dr. Yang is a sharing, caring friend—a bright light shining in the darkness.

Today, as in the past, Chung Syn's small home often is a haven for the needy. Widows, orphans, the visually handicapped, and the homeless feel free to visit the "blind lady preacher" when needing assistance. Whether suffering from a physical ailment or a broken heart, in need of counseling or a bed and a bowl of rice, no one is turned away empty-handed by Inchon's lady of mercy. Nor does anyone leave without first hearing about God's saving grace.

"None of us can work his or her way to heaven," she says, "for salvation is a free gift from the Lord. It isn't a question of *what* or *how much* we do for Him that counts. Only what Christ did for us on the Cross really matters." Invariably she quotes Ephesians 2:8–9: "By grace you have been saved, through faith—and this not from yourselves, it is the gift of God—not by works, so that no one can boast."

Chung Syn doesn't quibble about doctrinal differences or dwell on the dichotomy of beliefs that exists among Christians in Korea today. Instead she sticks to biblical truths. "After centuries of confusion," she explains, "some Christians still believe they must *do something* to make them worthy of going to heaven. They don't seem to understand that Christ paid for our sins on the Cross and that we have been forgiven—once and for all. Of course," she hastens to add, "a Christian's life should be fruitful. But good works must come as the consequence of gratitude and love, *not* from a sense of duty."

During the past several decades Christian churches have sprung up all over Korea. The Samil church of Inchon, which Dr. Yang founded and still pastors, is a classic example. Her congregation is steadily growing, both in number and in biblical knowledge. There, and wherever she speaks, audiences are moved by the clarity of Chung Syn's messages and her astounding knowledge of Scripture, much of which is committed to memory. Yet, in spite of these accomplishments, Chung Syn makes no claim to fame. Instead, she is a bit embarrassed by praise. "To God be the glory," she insists, "for the things He has done. Without Him I am nothing."

Just as Helen Keller awoke America, Dr. Yang has engaged in a one-woman crusade on behalf of Korea's visually handicapped. At times she has even battled government bureaucracy in an effort to win recognition for the blind. The results of her campaign have been most convincing. Quietly, and in Chung Syn's own inimitable way, she has contributed immeasurably to Korea's cultural revolution.

Today visually impaired Koreans enjoy a new status in society. Many have entered universities and are competing successfully on an academic level with sighted students—while Chung Syn, their predecessor, stands on the sidelines and cheers.

Perhaps you are wondering, as many have, whether Chung Syn is sorry for choosing a life of service rather than marriage to the man she loved.

"I have been much too busy to dwell on things that might have been," she says, "although at one time in my life it was a great temptation to let love and the desires of a young heart rule my head. Now, from the vantage point of maturity, I realize that all things did 'work together for good' in the end. No doubt the responsibilities of marriage and motherhood would have prevented me from devoting myself whole-heartedly to the work God called me to do.

"Today I can look back on happy memories of Sinbo and the past without regret or remorse. There is nothing as satisfying as being in partnership with the Lord. I kept my promise to Him, and in return He gave me a ministry that has been wonderfully fulfilling—as well as a host of orphan children to cuddle and care for.

"I wouldn't trade my experiences at the orphanage for anything! Each one of those precious, neglected youngsters needed love . . . security . . . a Christian home. And I needed them more than they knew! In their own charming ways they have more than fulfilled my maternal instincts. How many mothers, I wonder, have had the pleasure of caring for *dozens* of children—instead of only a few?

"Do I regret my decision? Of course not! Many undeserved blessings have been mine. God has brought wonderful people across my pathway, each one contributing something special and irrevocable in the way of happiness. Opportunities I never dreamed possible have come as sweet surprises.

"Little wonder the lyrics of that familiar chorus are so meaningful: 'How can I do less, Than give Him my best, And live for Him completely, After all He's done for me?'

"The Lord is everything to me—my King, Shepherd, Great Physician . . . and Savior. Whenever He calls, wherever He leads, I am ready to follow, and I look forward to singing someday with the angel choir:

> Amazing grace! how sweet the sound
> That saved a wretch like me!
> I once was lost, but now am found,
> *Was blind, but now I see!*"